Presented To:

_____

From:

_____

Date:

_____

The Lamb and the Seven-Sealed Scroll

DESTINY IMAGE BOOKS BY DR. RICHARD BOOKER

Discovering the Miracle of the Scarlet Thread in Every Book of the Bible

Celebrating Jesus in the Biblical Feasts

Radical Islam's War Against Israel, Christianity, and the West

Living in His Presence

The Miracle of the Scarlet Thread Revised

Blow the Trumpet in Zion

The Overcomers

AVAILABLE FROM DESTINY IMAGE PUBLISHERS

THE LAMB AND THE SEVEN-SEALED SCROLL

UNDERSTANDING THE BOOK OF REVELATION BOOK 2

Dr. Richard Booker

DESTINY IMAGE® PUBLISHERS, INC.

P.O. Box 310, Shippensburg, PA 17257-0310

"Promoting Inspired Lives

This book and all other Destiny Image, Revival Press, MercyPlace, Fresh Bread, Destiny Image Fiction, and Treasure House books are available at Christian bookstores and distributors worldwide.

For a U.S. bookstore nearest you, call **1-800-722-6774.**

For more information on foreign distributors, call **717-532-3040.**

Reach us on the Internet: **www.destinyimage.com.**

ISBN 13 TP: 978-0-7684-4075-1

ISBN 13 Ebook: 978-0-7684-8907-1

For Worldwide Distribution, Printed in the U.S.A.

1 2 3 4 5 6 7 8 / 16 15 14 13 12

Acknowledgments

TO Peggy, my wife and covenant partner of more than 45 years, who has faithfully served the Lord with me with unselfish love and support. Whatever I have been able to accomplish is because of her sacrifices and servant's heart. There are many great women in the world, but Peggy surpasses them all. She is the best Christian I know and a true overcomer who has her name written in the Lamb's Book of Life.

I also want to thank my friends at Destiny Image, especially Don Nori, for being faithful to his vision of "speaking to the purposes of God for this generation and for the generations to come."

I want to acknowledge two of my students, Angela James who gave so much of her time editing the manuscript and Mark Sessions who prepared the map and two charts for this series. Thank you both for your excellent work.

Contents

Preface

WHEN John was on the island of Patmos, the Lord gave him a revelation of Jesus, the exalted Son of Man, and of God's people overcoming satanic opposition before the throne of God. In spite of tremendous persecution, John saw "in the Spirit" that the faithful followers of the Lord were victorious. They overcame satan by the blood of the Lamb and the word of their testimony. Furthermore, John was given revelation to see the spiritual warfare in Heaven that was being played out on the earth. He saw the outcome of this spiritual battle as well as prophetic events that would take place in the end times before the coming of the Lord.

John saw that God would totally and completely destroy His enemies and resurrect His own people to live with Him forever in a new Heaven, a new earth and a New Jerusalem. Regardless of the trials and tribulations God's people must endure, our destiny is certain and sure. Jesus is returning, and we will rule and reign with Him in a world free of satan, sin, and death. In the challenging days ahead, believers can joyfully commit their souls to God, who is faithful to keep His Word of promise.

As John wrote at the end of his vision:

And I heard a loud voice from heaven saying, "Behold, the tabernacle of God is with men, and He will dwell with them, and they shall be His people. God Himself will be with them and be their God. And God will wipe away every tear from their eyes; there shall be no more death, nor sorrow, nor crying. There shall be no more pain, for the former things have passed away" (Revelation 21:3-4).

So the book of Revelation is not a book of doom and gloom, but of the victory of the Lamb and those who follow Him. The purpose of the Lord's revelation to John was to unveil or disclose to him what John could not know without divine assistance. The Lord gave John his vision to encourage and comfort his immediate readers as well as believers throughout the ages. What eventually became the book of Revelation was clearly intended to be understood by John and his first century readers.

However, with the passage of time, this book that God intended for us to understand became, without a doubt, the most mysterious book in the Bible. For almost 2,000 years, Christian scholars and everyday believers have tried to understand its message. Because the book of Revelation is an apocalyptic vision filled with otherworldly symbols and descriptions of strange creatures, God's people have not always agreed on its meaning. This has led to a number of different interpretations of John's words.

Since there are so many books written on John's revelation, with so many different interpretations, why would I feel burdened to add to the confusion? It was certainly not my intention to write a book on the book of Revelation. With more than 30 other books in print, I was ready to take a break from book writing. I wrote this book because there is an urgent need to explain John's Revelation with the following four points of view that have not been adequately included in most commentaries on the book of Revelation.

First, almost all books written to explain the book of Revelation are written with a Western cultural worldview rather than a biblical worldview. There are some exceptions. What I mean by this is that the writer interprets the book of Revelation through Western eyes rather than through the Hebraic eyes of a Middle Eastern person. John was not a Western theologian. He was a Jewish seer. This means that he understood and wrote his revelation in terms of his own history and culture. His history and culture is the Hebrew Bible—what Christians have always called the Old Testament. In this book, I prefer to use the phrase *Hebrew Bible.*

In order to understand the book of Revelation, we must read it through the eyes of a Jewish man rather than through the eyes of a Western theologian. For example, when John sees Jesus in Heaven, he describes Him in Jewish terms, not Western Christian terms. To get the fullest meaning of John's vision of Jesus, we need to know Jesus, the Jewish "Son of Man." To John, Jesus is the "Cloud Man" of the Book of Daniel.

Second, since the book of Revelation is the last book in the Bible, we must have a good understanding of all the other books in the Bible. We cannot understand the book of Revelation if we do not have a good understanding of Genesis through Jude, as well as some basic knowledge of the literature written between the Testaments, and of Greek mythology. We must not read John's revelation as if it were written in modern times isolated from the rest of the Bible. The best way to understand the book of Revelation is to begin with Genesis. For instance, when John explains the eternal home of believers in the last two chapters of the book of Revelation, he assumes that the reader will be familiar with the first two chapters of the book of Genesis.

Third, in order to understand the book of Revelation, we must interpret it according to the type of literature John used in writing it. John wrote the Revelation in an apocalyptic literary style. Apocalyptic literature flourished in the period of time in which John was writing. It has certain characteristics that John's readers readily understood. I explain these characteristics in Chapter 1. Because this is not a normal style of writing in our times, we have difficulty understanding and interpreting apocalyptic literature.

We have a tendency to interpret apocalyptic literature as if it were a literal story narrative, written chronologically like a Western textbook. Reading the book of Revelation as a Western textbook can clearly lead us to wrong conclusions regarding John's statements. For example, when John says that he saw an open door into Heaven and heard a voice calling him to Heaven, he did not mean that he saw a literal door and was literally taken to Heaven. He meant that God opened his spiritual eyes so that he could see realities in Heaven that he would not know otherwise. Physically, John never left Patmos.

Fourth, to properly understand the book of Revelation, we must know the historical context in which John wrote. Jesus gave John letters to write to seven literal congregations in the first century. Since the English word *church* means something different to modern readers than its biblical meaning, I use the word *congregation*, which is the more accurate meaning of the word. I could have used the words *assembly* or *community*. In a few instances, I use the word *Church* when referring to organized Christianity, such as the Roman Church or the Catholic Church. These congregations or communities were challenged every day to live out their new faith in a hostile environment in which their neighbors worshiped Greek gods and goddesses and Roman emperors, practiced gross immorality, and pressured them to compromise their faith and witness. They were faced with life and death decisions.

In addition, each of the cities where the seven congregations were located had their own unique physical circumstances that Jesus acknowledged in His letters. Without knowledge of their circumstances, spiritual and physical, it is impossible to understand why Jesus said what He said to the different congregations. For instance, if we do not know that

Laodicea had a drinking water problem, we cannot understand why Jesus preferred the believers to be cold or hot rather than lukewarm.

I have the greatest appreciation for scholars and ministers who have spent years studying the book of Revelation and have labored to help us understand its mysteries. While I present points of view in this book that most ministers and everyday believers might not be familiar with, I do not intend to be critical of what others have written or believe. We must all walk in love and humility and be gracious to one another, especially if we see things differently.

You may be challenged by some of my explanations that are contrary to your preconceived ideas and traditional teachings. You may not agree with everything I have written, and that is OK. What I desire to accomplish is to glorify our Lord, to encourage God's people to be steadfast and faithful as we face challenging days ahead, and to provide a fresh, exciting, and more balanced understanding of the book of Revelation. If I accomplish these goals, I would be most grateful to our Lord. May God's people be blessed and His name praised forever.

For ease of reading and understanding, the publisher has wisely organized my writing on the book of Revelation into a three-volume series entitled *Understanding the Book of Revelation*. Volume One is entitled *The Overcomers*. This volume begins with three chapters that are necessary for us to understand the historical events that prompted the Lord to send His letters to the seven congregations. In order to properly understand the Revelation, we must know the context in which it was written. I have also included a chapter on the literary style in which the book was written as well as a survey of the book of Revelation. I then explain the letters to the seven congregations within their historical, geographical, archeological and Hebraic context and perspective along with my view of their prophetic and personal significance. This background information is often missing or not adequately explained in most books on the Revelation, but is critical to understanding the Revelation. Volume One covers Revelation 1-3.

Volume Two is entitled *The Lamb and the Seven-Sealed Scroll*. This volume opens up with John's vision of Heaven and the throne room of God. John sees the greatest drama in human history when the Lamb of God takes the seven-sealed scroll and opens the seals. I then explain the events that follow, including the opening of the first six seals, God's seal of protection, Israelites and Jews, the multitude of the redeemed, the opening of the seventh seal, the mighty angel and the little book, the two witnesses, the proclamation of the Kingdom of God, and the war in Heaven and on earth. Volume Two covers Revelation 4-12. We will learn along the way that the book of Revelation actually ends with the close of Revelation 11. The rest of the information is an "instant replay" giving more details and different looks at the same information.

Volume Three is entitled *The Victorious Kingdom*. This volume includes an explanation of the two false messiahs, a preview of the end, preparing to blow the seventh trumpet-shofar, the blowing of the seventh trumpet-shofar, the destruction of the one-world religious and political systems, the second coming of Messiah, the Battle of Armageddon, the Messianic Kingdom, the New Heaven and New Earth and Paradise Restored. Volume Three covers Revelation 13-22.

These volumes are designed to be read along with the book of Revelation. Each discussion in the text is keyed to a specific chapter and verse in the book of Revelation. To get the most from the text, first read the information in the book of Revelation, and then read my explanations and comments in the books.

As I have already said, the Revelation is not a book about doom and gloom. While there are many hard things to read and much suffering in the book, Revelation is a book about God's faithfulness to Himself, His Word, and His people. It is about God defeating His enemies, and His people overcoming by the blood of the Lamb and the Word of their testimony. The outcome is certain and victory is sure. As you read the Revelation and this three-volume series, may the Lord encourage your heart that our God is sovereign over world conditions and is using them to move forward His awesome plan of redemption for His people. Do not be fearful in the dark days ahead. We will live with our Lord forever in the full manifestation of His blazing glory and dazzling beauty. We will look upon Him as He is, for we shall be like Him.

Let us make the following prayer from Jude 24-25 our own personal praise and worship to our God:

> *Now to Him who is able to keep you from stumbling* [fall-ing]*, and to present you faultless before the presence of His glory with exceeding joy, to God our Savior, who alone is wise, be glory and majesty, dominion and power, both now and forever. Amen.*

Chapter 1

The Throne Room of God in Heaven
Part 1

Review of Book 1, *The Overcomers*

IN Book 1, we learned that John wrote the Revelation as apocalyptic literature which was a recognized and acceptable form of literature in Bible times. Readers understood that writers of apocalyptic literature claim to have had a prophetic revelation from God that is supernatural. In this style of literature, the writer uses symbols and "otherworldly" visions and language to communicate heavenly realities to people living on the earth. This is not a common form of literature to modern readers. So we must keep this in mind as we continue our study of this mysterious and mystical book.

While most of the Book of Revelation is symbolic, it also contains literal messages to seven literal congregations in Asia Minor (modern Turkey) plus prophecy for our times. While first-century believers would have clearly understood John's message, it is not as clear to us today. This has led to many different interpretations of the Book of Revelation.

The event that seems to have prompted John to write his Revelation was associated with emperor worship. Rome established the imperial cult of emperor worship as a test of one's loyalty to the empire. They built temples, altars, and statues to the emperors throughout the empire and required the people to make sacrifices to the emperor.

Because the believers would not worship the emperor, they were persecuted. The Emperor Domitian built an imperial cult center in Ephesus which included an altar and a statue of Domitian. The local residents were required to bow down and offer sacrifices to the image.

Domitian insisted on being called "the lord God" and issued coins bearing his image and this phrase. Naturally, this created a crisis for the believers in Ephesus. Could they fix their sandals in front of the statue as a way of bowing down to the image without actually worshiping Domitian?

Jewish and Christian leaders said "No, we cannot even pretend to worship the beast even though we don't really mean it." To refuse to bow down to the image meant persecution, death, or exile. People needed some assurance that God knew their situation and had not forsaken them.

In view of this, the Lord gave John a prophetic vision with prophetic messages to the seven congregations. Each message would be read to the other congregations to praise them, warn them, and encourage them. John would then explain in apocalyptic terms future events describing the battle between good and evil until the coming of the Son of Man to set up the Kingdom of God on the earth. This is the background we must know in order to understand the Book of Revelation. If you have not read *The Overcomers* (Book 1 of this series) I encourage you to do so as it gives the background for the Book of Revelation as well as the Lord's letters to the seven congregations.

THE THRONE ROOM OF GOD IN HEAVEN
(REVELATION 4:1-3)

In Revelation 4 John uses apocalyptic language to describe a spiritual experience in which he has a vision of Heaven. In his spiritual state, John sees the throne room of God in all its glory and beauty and all of Heaven worshiping God. In this chapter, we will study John's statement about an open door to Heaven and his first glimpse of the throne room of God. We will continue with this subject in the next chapter.

The Open Door to Heaven (verse 1)

After receiving the prophetic messages to the seven congregations, the scene moves from Earth to Heaven, where John sees a door open. Speaking in apocalyptic language, this is not a literal door but a prophetic door of revelation. All of John's readers would have understood his statement in this way. (See Book 1 for an explanation of apocalyptic literature.)

John wants us to understand that he is going to receive a vision of Heaven that can only come by spiritual revelation from God Himself. He is going to be privileged to see what is happening in Heaven and then record that for the believers who are confronted with the throne of the imperial cult.

But the revelation is not only for believers in the seven congregations; it is for believers of all time who struggle with the challenge and heartache of seeing men and governments exalt themselves in the place of God. What we see on the earth is not the reality. The reality is what we see in Heaven. We just need the spiritual revelation to see it, and John gives it to us.

John hears a voice speaking to him and says it was like a trumpet-shofar. He uses the same phrase in Revelation 1:10. John was used to the voice of the Lord sounding like the sound of a trumpet-shofar. When the Lord brought the Hebrews out of Egypt, the Lord spoke to them through the sound of the trumpet-shofar (see Exod. 19:13-19). The people were so frightened by the whole experience that they asked Moses for the Lord not to speak to them directly again (see Exod. 20:18-19).

So one way the Lord continued to speak to them was through the use of trumpets-shofars (see Num. 10:1-10). When John heard the voice of the Lord, he heard it as the sound of a trumpet-shofar. This was part of the history and heritage of his people in hearing the Word of the Lord. He knew what it meant, and it certainly got his attention.

The voice told John to come to Heaven to receive the spiritual revelation of the next things the Lord wanted to show him. There are two statements here to consider; the first is the statement commanding John to come to Heaven.

Ministers who believe and proclaim a pre-tribulation rapture interpret this verse and command to *"Come up here"* to mean that John is representing believers who are raptured or caught up to Heaven at this time before the beginning of the tribulation. Scholars and serious students of the Book of Revelation certainly have the right to their studied interpretation of the Book. We should bless, love, and respect those who have different views than ours and not be dogmatic where there is a difference of opinions.

Furthermore, believers who have only been taught the pre-tribulation rapture may be surprised to learn that not everyone shares this interpretation of this specific Scripture. We need to be humble and teachable. When we read or hear a teaching that is contrary to what we have always believed, we should be like the Bereans who searched the Scriptures daily to discover truth (see Acts 17:11).

As I stated in the first paragraph of this chapter, it is important to keep in mind that the Book of Revelation is written in an apocalyptic writing style. This means we should not interpret this book too literally. Now this may be a shock to some, but John was not literally raptured to Heaven. I know, this may really sound upsetting if this is the only interpretation you have been taught and accepted. God bless all well-meaning godly ministers who teach this view.

It just didn't happen. John is using apocalyptic language to say that he is going to receive a prophetic word from God that is supernatural. He is using symbolic language to describe it. There was no literal door and no literal rapture of John's body to Heaven at this time.

John had a spiritual vision of Heaven but he was still on the earth at Patmos. Physically, he didn't go anywhere. Since he was not literally raptured, this verse cannot possibly suggest a literal rapture of believers to Heaven at this time in God's great end-time chronology of events. Those who do so are certainly making a good faith effort to understand and interpret this verse. I applaud them but this interpretation turns an apocalyptic statement into a literal event that simply cannot be supported by this verse. I pray that you will have "ears to hear."

For example, in Revelation 17:3, John says that the Spirit carried him into the wilderness. Should we interpret this to mean that believers are also raptured into the wilderness? In Revelation 21:10 John says that the Spirit carried him away to a great and high mountain. Should we interpret this to mean that believers are also raptured to a great and high mountain? I think you get the point.

I explained in Book 1 that in apocalyptic literature it was common for the author to put someone else's name on his writing. This was a famous deceased person to whom the writer wanted to attribute his ideas. This type of writing was referred to as *pseudepigrapha*. According to the dictionary this is a word meaning "falsely ascribed or attributed." It is a spurious work attributed to a biblical character. Today we would say that the author used a pen name. Except in this case, the pen name was the name of a real person.

There were numerous *pseudepigrapha* written between 200 B.C. and A.D. 200. One of the most popular written between the testaments was the Book of Enoch, which I referred to in Book 1. Enoch did not write the book bearing his name, and we don't know who did write it. The

Book of Enoch was widely quoted by both Jews and early followers of Jesus. I have noted that Jude 14-15 quotes the Book of Enoch.

While the Book of Enoch was not included in the Bible, it provides a good example of how writers in the time of John expressed themselves in apocalyptic language. People who read the Book of Enoch in its time understood it for what it was—an apocalyptic vision. They did not take it literally. I have included a brief quotation from the Book of Enoch so we can read for ourselves this very unique style of writing and see how it is similar to John's words.

Here is how Enoch describes his "catching up" to Heaven:

> And the vision was shown to me thus: Behold in the vision clouds invited me and a mist summoned me, and the course of the stars and the lightings sped and hastened me, and the wind in the vision caused me to fly and lifted me upward, and bore me into heaven.…And the Lord called me with His own mouth, and said to me, "Come hither, Enoch, and hear My word." And one of the holy ones came to me and waked me, and He made me rise up and approach the door: and I bowed my face downwards.[1]

We can see the similarity in language. Enoch did not literally go to Heaven and neither did John. John has a prophetic vision in which God opens a prophetic door to him and invites him to enter the door. Literally, John is in prison on the Isle of Patmos. Spiritually, he has a vision of the throne room of God, heavenly worship, and the war between good and evil down through the ages. John sees the final victory of God through the Son of Man, Jesus the Messiah who is the Lion of the Tribe of Judah, the Lamb of God, who gave His life for our sins so that we can be reconciled to God and live as overcomers.

The second statement to consider is the one in which the Lord says He will show John *"things which must take place after this."*

Scholars who interpret the Book of Revelation literally see chapters 4-22 as the chronological order of the Book of Revelation. There is certainly a chronological order to some events John describes. But when John says, *"things which must take place after this"* he is using apocalyptic language to refer to the next part of his prophetic vision. He does not necessarily mean the next events but the next part of his vision. The point is not to read in too literal an interpretation of spiritual language. There are successive chronological events in the Book of Revelation. We just need to be cautious and not dogmatic in interpreting "otherworldly" language and symbols too literally.

The Throne Set in Heaven (verses 2-3)

To emphasize that he is having a prophetic vision, John once again says that he is *"in the Spirit."* John uses this phrase four times (see Rev. 1:10; 4:2; 17:3; 21:10). The reader would understand John to be saying that the Holy Spirit was giving him additional spiritual revelation that he could not possibly know by his own human intellect or imagination. These "in the Spirit" statements are the order for understanding the Book of Revelation.

In his spiritual state, John sees a throne in Heaven and One sitting on the throne. This "One" is the Creator of all things (see Rev. 4:8). He is not the generic "god of the world" nor is He the god of any religion outside of the Bible. He is Yahveh, the Judeo-Christian God of Abraham, Isaac, and Jacob; He is the God of Israel. The Lord Himself makes this claim as we learn in Isaiah:

> *Thus says the LORD, the King of Israel, and His Redeemer, the LORD of hosts: "I am the First and I am the Last; besides Me there is no God"* (Isaiah 44:6).

Because God is so glorious in His appearance, no one can see Him in the fullness of His blazing glory and dazzling beauty. Surely we can understand that the creature cannot see the Creator in all of His fullness. If we did, we would all die.

A natural example we can all understand is that no one can look directly into the sun without seeing spots or going blind. We have to turn our eyes away from the sun or look at it with special glasses or through dark clouds. This is what the Bible means when it says that God is invisible or cannot be seen (see 1 Tim. 1:17; John 1:18).

In the Hebrew Bible, we are told that God *spoke to Moses face to face* (Exod. 33:11). This is a Hebraic figure of speech. The writer wants us to understand that when Moses approached God, he was not in a spiritual trance or having a vision like John, but was fully conscious and aware that he was in God's presence. It does not mean that Moses literally saw God's face.

Later in the same chapter, Moses pleaded with God to show him His glory. The Lord then told Moses that no one could see His face, meaning the fullness of His glory, and live. (See Exodus 33:18-23.)

So when the Bible talks about someone seeing the Lord, it does not mean that the person sees Him in bodily form. It means that the person sees a manifestation of God which the person describes in heavenly terms of majestic divine glory and beauty.

For example, Exodus reads:

> *Then Moses went up, also Aaron, Nadab, and Abihu, and seventy of the elders of Israel, and they saw the God of Israel. And there was under His feet as it were a paved work of sapphire stone, and it was like the very heavens in its clarity* (Exodus 24:9-10).

The prophet Micaiah described his vision of the Lord in this way:

> *Then Micaiah said, "Therefore hear the word of the LORD: I saw the LORD sitting on His throne, and all the*

host of heaven standing by, on His right hand and on His left" (1 Kings 22:19).

Isaiah described a vision of the Lord similar to John's. Isaiah said:

> *In the year that King Uzziah died, I saw the Lord sitting on a throne, high and lifted up, and the train [glory] of His robe filled the temple. Above it stood seraphim; each one had six wings: with two he covered his face, with two he covered his feet, and with two he flew. And one cried to another and said: "Holy, holy, holy is the LORD of hosts; the whole earth is full of His glory"* (Isaiah 6:1-3).

The prophet Ezekiel said that the heavens were opened to him and that he *"saw visions of God"* (Ezek. 1:1). In the rest of the chapter, Ezekiel describes all he saw using language similar to Moses, Micaiah, Isaiah, and John (see Ezek. 1). In his vision of Heaven, Enoch said that he saw a throne with "the Great Glory" sitting on it.[2]

As with others who have had a true vision of Heaven, John does not describe God in a definable form but in terms humans can understand. John speaks of God's blazing glory and dazzling beauty as brilliant gemstones of jasper and sardius (or carnelian).

Jasper was one of the stones in the high priest's breastplate (see Exod. 28:20). Jasper is also mentioned later in Revelation to describe the brilliant, pure light of the glory of God; it is called a *"precious stone"* that is as *"clear as crystal"* (Rev. 21:11). From a spiritual standpoint, we can say that jasper symbolizes the pure holiness of God.

While we don't know the exact color of the jasper that John sees, because it is crystal clear, we can think of it today as resembling a brilliant, sparkling diamond. Both the wall and the first foundation of the New Jerusalem are made of jasper (see Rev. 21:18-19). Because jasper is said to be crystal clear, the glory of God can be seen emanating everywhere throughout the New Jerusalem, the city God has prepared as the eternal home of His people. Praise God!

Sardius (or carnelian) is a beautiful red like a ruby. Sardius was also one of the stones in the high priest's breastplate (see Exod. 28:17). It is listed as the sixth foundation of the New Jerusalem (see Rev. 21:20). Whereas the jasper symbolizes the holiness of God, we can understand that the deep blood-red sardius is a spiritual symbol of the necessity of redemption through the blood of an innocent substitutionary sacrifice for sin.

In addition to these gorgeous stones, John also sees an emerald or green-colored rainbow around God's throne. The way John describes it, the rainbow is a full circle around the throne. The full circle symbolizes eternity, much like the wedding ring symbolizes the sacredness of the marriage covenant between a man and a woman. Exodus 28:17 lists emerald as one of the stones in the breastplate of the high priest. It is also the fourth foundation of the wall of the New Jerusalem (see Rev. 21:19).

On several occasions, I have seen the full-circle rainbow from the air. It is a magnificent and truly spectacular sight. The rainbow is a sign of God's covenant of life, as we learn in Genesis 9:12-17. Through his vision of God's throne, John is given an apocalyptic message that a holy God has entered into an everlasting blood covenant with His people through the innocent substitutionary sacrifice of His Son who gave His life for the sins of mankind.

Furthermore, John's vision contrasts the heavenly throne of God to the earthly throne of the emperor and imperial cult worship. To the people living under Roman rule, the majesty and splendor of the throne of the emperor represented the most powerful ruler in the world. The emperor was a "god" to be feared and obeyed without question. You proved your loyalty to the emperor by sacrificing to him at his temple or statue and altar. The believers were faced with this challenge and crisis.

The Roman emperor controlled most of the world. His power was absolute and his riches immeasurable. He could do whatever he wanted.

He could kill your body but not your soul. Yet his power and majesty could not even compare to the sovereign rule of God over all of His creation. Caesar's power, wealth, and glory, as represented by his throne, were nothing compared to the blazing glory and dazzling beauty of the throne of God.

Furthermore, the emperor would have no power at all unless the Almighty allowed for it. We learn this in the Gospel records in the Bible. When Pilate threatened Jesus with crucifixion, Jesus said to him, *"You could have no power at all against Me unless it had been given you from above..."* (John 19:11).

The vision of the throne room of God would certainly comfort the believers and assure them that God alone was the sovereign Lord and Master of the universe. He alone was to be feared and obeyed. He alone was to be worshiped. In time, He would judge the arrogance of the imperial cult and set His people in the place of honor. Therefore, the believers to whom John wrote learned not to fear those who ruled over them in this world. John's message applies to believers in the world today; we should pray for those in authority over us; but ultimately our lives are in God's hands, not those of evil rulers.

God alone is the supreme sovereign over His creation. And He has promised eternal rewards to His people who overcome the temptations of this world. While it is possible for evil rulers to kill our bodies, God will raise us up with new bodies to live with Him forever. As Paul writes:

> *But if the Spirit of Him who raised Jesus from the dead dwells in you, He who raised Christ* [Messiah] *from the dead will also give life to your mortal bodies through His Spirit who dwells in you* (Romans 8:11).

All the Caesars are dead but Jesus, the Son of Man, lives! Earthly leaders only rule for a short time but God rules forever. He alone is to be feared, praised, and worshiped.

While God is going to pour out His wrath on the ungodly, He has an everlasting covenant of life for His people purchased for us through the substitutionary blood sacrifice of Jesus. As Paul wrote to the believers at Thessalonica:

> For God did not appoint us to wrath, but to obtain salvation through our Lord Jesus Christ [Yeshua the Messiah], who died for us, that whether we wake or sleep, we should live together with Him. Therefore comfort each other and edify one another, just as you also are doing (1 Thessalonians 5:9-11).

Hallelujah!

REVIEW QUESTIONS

1. Write a summary of what you have learned in this lesson. Write the summary in clear, concise words as if you were going to present it to another person.

2. Write an explanation of how you can apply what you have learned in this lesson to your life.

3. Share what you have learned with your family, friends, and members of your study group.

ENDNOTES

1. The Book of Enoch 14:8-9; 24-25; www.sacredtexts.com; accessed December 7, 2011.

2. The Book of Enoch 14:20; see 14:18-25; www.sacredtexts.com; accessed December 7, 2011.

Chapter 2

The Throne Room of God in Heaven
Part 2

I N the previous chapter, we learned that John saw an open door to Heaven. Then he heard a voice like the sound of a trumpet-shofar telling him to *"Come up here...."* He would then be shown what *"must take place after this"* (Rev. 4:1).

We must keep in mind that John wrote in an apocalyptic style of literature that was common in his day. The writer used symbols and "otherworldly" visions to communicate heavenly realities to people living on the earth. Just as we read various types of literature differently, people who read apocalyptic literature did not take the writer literally but sought to understand the prophetic and spiritual truth being presented.

This is how we must interpret the Book of Revelation. While the Lord did write to seven literal congregations, and He is literally returning, most of the Book of Revelation communicates this symbolically. John's first-century readers understood his symbols and their meanings. As people separated by time, language, history, and literary style from these early believers, we must do our best to understand John's words as they understood them.

When John said he saw a door open to Heaven, his contemporary readers did not think that he meant a literal door, but a prophetic door. God was going to allow John to see spiritually into the throne room of God.

When the Lord opened this prophetic door, He invited John to enter through it. Again, John's readers did not think he was physically transported to Heaven; they understood that he was describing a prophetic vision.

John was physically in exile on Patmos. He was not raptured to Heaven. As stated in the previous chapter those who believe in a pre-tribulation rapture explain that this verse teaches that John represents the Church being raptured or "caught up" to Heaven before the tribulation. The problem with using this verse to teach a pre-tribulation rapture is that John was not raptured. This interpretation does not take into consideration the apocalyptic nature of the Book of Revelation. It reads it too literally.

Furthermore, when John was told that God would show him things that must take place after this, He did not necessarily mean things that would take place after this in chronological time. He meant the next part of his prophetic vision. While some of the Book of Revelation is chronological, other parts simply describe John receiving further prophetic insight, or as I will explain later, "instant replays," from the Lord. This misunderstanding of John's words is also a result of interpreting the Book of Revelation too literally. To repeat, the Book of Revelation is not a Western story to be interpreted the way we interpret Western books.

What John sees is the throne room of God. John does not describe God in a definable form, but sees a manifestation of the glory of God. John sees God as brilliant gemstones of jasper and sardius surrounded by an emerald-color rainbow circle. The crystal-clear jasper is a symbol of God's purity while the deep red sardius is a symbol of the necessity of blood sacrifice for sin. The emerald-color rainbow circle is a symbol of God's covenant of everlasting life with those who accept His redemption through Jesus. This is a visual picture of the blood of the everlasting covenant.

Once John gets his spiritual eyes focused, he notices that there are people and special beings around God's throne who give Him constant worship and praise. Let's now look with John as he further reveals his vision to us.

THE THRONE ROOM OF GOD IN HEAVEN
(REVELATION 4:4-11)

The 24 Elders (verse 4)

Around the throne of God, John sees 24 elders clothed in white. They are also sitting on thrones and have gold crowns on their heads. Who are these 24 elders and what are they doing around the throne of God?

Bible scholars have different views regarding the identity of the 24 elders. Some believe they are a special group of angels while others see them as the representatives of the redeemed of all humanity. We don't want to lose our focus by arguing over our differences and we should be gracious toward those who have a different interpretation of unexplained symbols in the Book of Revelation. At the same time, we should do our best to understand the meaning of what John sees in his vision.

While John does not tell us the identity of these elders, those reading his words understood his meaning. So what would they understand him to be saying to them? If we understand John's vision as apocalyptic literature and consider its historical and Hebraic setting, I believe we can know who the 24 elders represent.

Since John is a Jew, we would look to the Hebrew Scriptures for the answer. We are not disappointed. When King David was making his plans for Solomon to build the Temple, David realized there were so many in the priestly line that they couldn't all serve at the same time.

David's solution to this dilemma was to divide them into 24 groups or orders with each group represented by a single priest. When the group met to serve there was one high priest and 24 chief priests. Together they represented the whole priesthood as well as the entire nation of Israel. David organized the Levites in the same way. You can read this for yourself in First Chronicles 24. Each group was assigned a specific time to serve at the Temple for two weeks each year. The selection and order of service was determined by casting lots (see 1 Chron. 24:5).

King David also appointed singers and musicians to prophesy day and night with harps, lyres, and cymbals. He divided them into 24 groups as well. (See First Chronicles 25.) David instructed the Levites to *stand every morning to thank and praise the Lord, and likewise at evening*" (1 Chron. 23:30). He instructed the singers and musicians in the *songs of the LORD*" (1 Chron. 25:7). David's tabernacle, and later the Temple, was filled with praise and worship to God.

This background information should give us a good idea of who the 24 elders represent. In the Bible, numbers often have symbolic meanings. Scholars understand that the number 12 can symbolize government or leadership and can be a representative number. Furthermore, the Bible refers to Jews and non-Jewish believers as the priests of God (see Exod. 19:6; 1 Pet. 2:9; Rev. 1:6; 5:10).

John's revelation gives us further information to clarify the identity of the 24 elders. The Son of Man promised the overcomers that He would give them the crown of life (see Rev. 2:10), cloth them in white garments (see Rev. 3:5) and allow them to sit with Him on His throne (see Rev. 3:21). This is how John describes the 24 elders. They are clothed in white, which symbolizes their purity, they are sitting with the Lord on their own thrones which symbolize their royal position as

Kingdom people, and they are wearing gold crowns on their head. They are constantly offering praise and worship to God and singing the new song of the redeemed. Sound familiar?

The Greek word translated into English as crown is *stephanos*.[1] It does not mean the crown of a sovereign king but that of a victor, like the winner in a sporting event receives the victor's crown. Only the Lord wears the crown of the sovereign King (see Rev. 19:12). But His people wear the crown of the overcomer.

In his apocalyptic vision, John sees the believers in the seven congregations receiving the promises the Son of Man gave to those who overcame (see Rev. 2:7,11,17,26; 3:5,12,21; 21:7). He writes this to them to encourage them not to "fix their sandals" at the altar and statue to the emperor. If they overcome they will receive the promised blessings. Hallelujah!

The Caesars organized formal emperor worship festivals with choirs, singing, dancing, and sacrifices. It was quite a spectacle as the whole community expressed their loyalty and allegiance to the empire. It was a joyous festival of celebration for sure. Yet, it paled in comparison to the praise and worship of God's people in Heaven. The believers in the seven congregations to whom John wrote should not feel "left out" of the worldly excitement accompanying emperor worship in their towns. If they overcame, they would have a celebration in Heaven to look forward to; it would be pure and holy and much more exciting. Plus, it would last forever.

This prophetic vision was specifically to the people facing the challenge and crisis of the imperial cult of emperor worship. But his vision is certainly relevant to all of God's people throughout history who have stood firm and resisted compromising their faith even when it meant persecution and martyrdom. As with God's people in times past, we too overcome by the blood of the Lamb and the word of our testimony (see Rev. 12:11). This is certainly an encouraging word for believers today who live in an increasingly anti-God world.

When taking everything into consideration, the 24 elders are seen with Jesus the High Priest (see Rev. 5) and represent the 12 tribes of Israel and the 12 apostles of our Lord who began the Jewish-Jesus movement that was later embraced by Gentiles and became known as Christianity. Together, they represent the company of the redeemed of all humanity (Jews and ingrafted non-Jewish believers) seen in Heaven offering constant praise and worship to our God. Revelation 21:12,14 add to this understanding and say that the 12 gates in the New Jerusalem have the names of the 12 tribes of the children of Israel while the foundations of the city have the names of the 12 apostles.

Rumblings in Heaven (verse 5)

John sees the awesome and frightening power of God around His throne which we would certainly expect for the Creator of the universe. He mentions lightnings, thunderings, voices (loud rumblings) and seven lamps of fire (see Rev. 4:5). Anyone who has ever been in a violent thunderstorm can appreciate the power and force of what John sees. It can be terrifying. In the Bible, these phenomena accompany the presence of God and symbolize His awesome power and majesty. I can guarantee you that the emperor did not have such an entourage surrounding him.

When God revealed Himself at Mount Sinai, His presence was announced with thunderings, lightnings, a thick cloud, smoke and fire, and a long, loud frightening blast of the shofar that got louder and louder. The whole mountain shook violently. The people were terrified. (See Exodus 19:16-19.) Wouldn't you be fainthearted if you were there?

Throughout the Book of Revelation, these phenomena are manifested when God concludes His series of judgments. For example, when the seventh seal is opened God announces the coming judgments with thunderings, lightnings, noises (rumblings), and an earthquake (see Rev. 8:5). This is repeated when the seventh trumpet is sounded (see Rev. 11:19). In addition to the thunderings, lightnings, rumblings, and the earthquake, there is great hail. John records the same phenomena with the seventh bowl judgment and adds that the earthquake is the largest the earth has ever experienced (see Rev. 16:18).

Our God is an awesome God. No earthly ruler, no matter how much power and control he has, can compare to the greatness of our God. He alone is worthy of our awe and our praise and worship. In their arrogance, ancient emperors and Caesars and modern would-be dictators think they are in control. They laugh at God and His people. Yet they are nothing compared to our God. He will have the last laugh, as we learn in the Book of Psalms:

> *He who sits in the heavens shall laugh; the Lord shall hold them in derision. Then He shall speak to them in His wrath, and distress them in His deep displeasure: "Yet I have set My King on My holy hill of Zion. I will declare the decree: The LORD has said to Me, 'You are My Son, today I have begotten You. Ask of Me, and I will give You the nations for Your inheritance, and the ends of the earth for Your possession. You shall break them with a rod of iron; You shall dash them to pieces like a potter's vessel'"* (Psalm 2:4-9).

For those who may be tempted to "fix their sandals" before the altars of the anti-God government and world system, don't do it. The arrogant leaders of the nations of our world who seek to rule without God are neither to be feared nor admired. They are to be pitied. They come and go and only last a short time. But our God is the Ancient of Days. His days are without number and His Kingdom is everlasting. Our God in Heaven will soon break the power of every puny dictator and foolish council of nations. They will all soon bow to Him and acknowledge that our God is God and He alone is sovereign.

As we also learn in Psalms:

All the ends of the world shall remember and turn to the
LORD, and all the families of the nations shall worship
before You. For the kingdom is the Lord's, and He rules
over the nations (Psalm 22:27-28).

In addition to the natural phenomena surrounding the throne of God, John also sees seven lamps of fire burning before the throne of God. In this instance, we don't have to interpret what John means by this symbol because he tells us. He says that the seven lamps of fire are the seven Spirits of God.

In Revelation 1:4, the seven Spirits of God send greetings to the seven congregations. In Revelation 3:1, Jesus told the believers at Sardis that He had the seven Spirits of God. In discussing these verses, I mentioned that the number seven, when connected to God, means perfection. The seven Spirits of God connects to Isaiah 11:2 and Zechariah 4:2-6. The phrase refers to the Holy Spirit or as John would say in Hebrew, *Ruach HaKodesh*.[2]

We cannot see the Holy Spirit unless the Spirit is embodied in some way such as in the form of a dove when Jesus was baptized (see Matt. 3:16) and in the tongues of fire in Acts 2:3. In John's vision, the Holy Spirit is manifested through the seven lamps of fire.

The Four Living Creatures (verses 6-11)

John continues to describe his prophetic vision in apocalyptic language and mentions a sea of glass before the throne of God. He says it is like crystal. He did not mean that he saw a literal sea. He was using figurative language to describe the floor in front of God's throne. He is trying to explain the limitless splendor and riches of God in contrast to that of the emperors.

When Moses, Aaron, his sons, and the 70 elders of Israel approached God on Mount Sinai, they saw something similar under the feet of God. Exodus reads:

> *and they saw the God of Israel. And there was under His feet as it were a paved work of sapphire stone, and it was like the very heavens in its clarity* (Exodus 24:10).

In Ezekiel's vision of Heaven, he also mentions an expanse which he describes as *"an awesome crystal"* (Ezek. 1:22).

In ancient times, including the New Testament era, crystal-clear glass was rare. As a result, crystal was very expensive. The Romans considered crystal a luxury item that only the super wealthy could afford. Of course the emperors had crystal, but even to them, it was a symbol of wealth and extravagance. By saying that God's throne sits on a sea of crystal-clear glass, John is making a big point for the believers to whom he is writing. He is saying that the throne of God far surpasses that of any earthly ruler including the emperor. Therefore, don't "fix your sandals" before the altar to Caesar.

This is certainly a word for us today. The glory of God that believers will enjoy in Heaven makes the riches of this world pale in comparison. Whatever the world can offer us in the way of material riches is not worth having if it means we must compromise or bow to the anti-God system to get it or keep it. God's riches far surpass anything this world can offer us. He has an infinite supply of spectacular splendor waiting for us to enjoy on the other side.

John also sees four "otherworldly" beings around the throne of God. The English language translation refers to them as four living creatures or beings. Who are these strange beings and what are they doing around the throne of God?

Because John is a Jewish visionary, we find the answer in the Hebrew Bible where we learn that God created special beings called the *"host of heaven"* (Neh. 9:6). We know them by their more common name, *angels.* Angels are mentioned throughout the Hebrew Bible as well as the New Testament and in all ancient cultures.

God created angels before He created human beings and endowed them with supernatural abilities far beyond those He gave to humans. Angels are personal beings God created for the purpose of serving Him and people. We cannot see angels with our natural eyes unless they reveal themselves to us. Many people claim that they have seen angels. They are very active in our world, we just are not aware of their presence and activities.

Because God so transcends humans, it is not feasible for Him to directly reveal Himself to us unless He appears in a veiled way, as He did at Mount Sinai. In our fallen human condition, we simply cannot stand in the direct presence of our Creator. The gap between the infinite Creator and the finite creature is too great. Angels, therefore, assist God in ministering to people. When necessary, they connect Heaven to Earth as God's messengers communicating His plans and will to mankind, executing His plans and will on the earth, announcing and carrying out His judgments, praising and worshiping God, etc.

Two of the highest orders of angles mentioned in the Bible are called *cherubim* and *seraphim.* The etymology of the word cherubim is not clear. Because of their ministry in the presence of God, scholars have understood the word to mean "holiness." We first learn about cherubim in the Garden of Eden where God placed them at the entrance to prevent Adam and Eve from eating from the tree of life (see Gen. 3:24).

God instructed Moses to make a sculpture of two cherubim and affix them to the Ark of the Covenant where God would meet with Moses in the Holy of Holies in the tabernacle. God's glory appeared between the cherubim above the mercy seat. Cherubim were also embroidered on the curtains of the tabernacle and later in the Temple. In his apocalyptic vision, Ezekiel described four living creatures similar to what John saw in his revelation (see Ezek. 1 and 10).

Considering all the references to cherubim, they are the living "Chariots of God" carrying Him when He appears to humans. They serve as guardians of God's throne and His presence. Of course God does not need any special beings to guard His throne or presence but He has chosen to create cherubim for this purpose so He can connect with human beings.

The word *seraphim* comes from a Hebrew word, *saraph*, which means "to burn or burning ones." They are mentioned in Isaiah 6:2, quoted earlier. I quote it again here for your convenience. Isaiah said:

> *In the year that King Uzziah died, I saw the Lord sitting on a throne, high and lifted up, and the train [glory] of His robe filled the temple. Above it stood seraphim; each one had six wings: with two he covered his face, with two he covered his feet, and with two he flew. And one cried to another and said: "Holy, holy, holy is the LORD of hosts; the whole earth is full of His glory"* (Isaiah 6:1-3).

Isaiah's description of the seraphim is similar to the four living creatures John describes. John says that each living creature has six wings and is full of eyes. One has the face of a lion, one the face of a calf, one the face of a man, and one the face of a flying eagle.

It would be easy to speculate at length on the meaning of the symbolism of their appearance (their faces and wings), but the important consideration is the function of the seraphim. In Hebraic thinking, function is more important than form. So what is their function? It seems that their sole purpose is to glorify God through continuous praise and worship. They are God's praise and worship leaders in Heaven. Along with the cherubim, they are God's highest order of angels who lead all of Heaven in glorifying God for His greatness as expressed in the beauty of His holiness.

While the English translation of words is slightly different, their worship is basically the same as what Isaiah saw and heard in his vision.

We are blessed that John records this heavenly worship for us: *"Holy, holy, holy, Lord God Almighty, who was and is and is to come!"* (Rev. 4:8).

In a deeply moving song she copyrighted in 1986, Elisheva Shomron put these powerful words to music. Below are the Hebrew lyrics with the English translation in brackets:

Kadosh, kadosh, kadosh [Holy, holy, holy],
Adonai Elohim Tz'va'ot [Lord God of Hosts]...
Asher hayah [who was]
V'hoveh [and who is]
V' yavo [and who is to come][3]

This awesome worship to God continues with the seraphim giving glory and honor and thanks to the Lord. The 24 elders watching all of this cannot simply be idle observers. Who could just stand by while all of this glorious worship is taking place? They fall on their faces before God, cast their crowns before His throne, and declare:

You are worthy, O Lord, to receive glory and honor and
power; for You created all things, and by Your will they
exist and were created (Revelation 4:11).

May we do the same as we contemplate the greatness of our Father in Heaven.

Whenever the Roman emperor would begin his procession in a parade of triumph, the crowds would line the streets and greet him saying, "You are worthy." As we have learned previously, Domitian added the phrase "our Lord and God" to the greeting.

In our current passage, John encourages the believers faced with emperor worship to recognize that God alone is worthy. He alone is the Lord God. He alone has created everything and sustains everything by the Word of His power. No Roman emperor ever created anything out of nothing. They are born, they live, and they die. But the Lord God Almighty created everything by the power of His spoken Word. He alone transcends time and space. He was, He is, and He is to come (see Rev. 4:8). Hallelujah!

The Caesars of Rome and the arrogant leaders of our world today are nothing compared to the Creator of the universe. In light of this glorious heavenly vision, believers should not bow to the anti-God governments and leaders of our world. The One True God will soon pour out His judgments on them until they bow to Him.

When John says that the 24 elders cast their crowns before the throne, he is using symbolic language to say that they are acknowledging that God alone is worthy of their praise and worship. Because of God's greatness and goodness, His power, His grace, and His mercy, they were able to overcome. May we do the same!

REVIEW QUESTIONS

1. Write a summary of what you have learned in this lesson. Write the summary in clear, concise words as if you were going to present it to another person.

2. Write an explanation of how you can apply what you have learned in this lesson to your life.

3. Share what you have learned with your family, friends, and members of your study group.

ENDNOTES

1. Biblesoft's New Exhaustive Strong's Numbers and Concordance with Expanded Greek-Hebrew Dictionary. CD-ROM. Biblesoft, Inc. and International Bible Translators, Inc. (1994, 2003, 2006) s.v. "stephanos," (NT 4735).

2. *Blue Letter Bible,* Dictionary and Word Search for *"holy" and "spirit"* (Strong's 6944 and 7307), 1996-2011, <http://www.blueletterbible.org/search/translationResults. cfm?Criteria=Holy+Spirit&t=KJV> (accessed May 11, 2011).

3. Sing to the Lord a New Song – songs from the Feast of Tabernacles- SJJ Productions, Kalkstrand Finland compilation copyright 1999. Page 79

Chapter 3

The Lamb and the Seven-Sealed Scroll

IN the previous chapter, I explained how John used apocalyptic language to describe a prophetic vision of Heaven. He was not literally raptured to Heaven as is popularly taught but was given a spiritual view of the throne room of God. A prophetic door of revelation was opened to John. It was not a literal door but a spiritual door. John was physically in a prison on the Isle of Patmos but was "in the Spirit" (see Rev. 1:10; 4:2). This simply means that the Holy Spirit opened John's spiritual eyes to see a heavenly scene he would not be able to see otherwise.

God's people have similar experiences when meditating on God's Word. Just because we have a spiritual revelation from Heaven doesn't mean that we are literally in Heaven. We might be mowing the yard, driving on the freeway, taking a shower, reading God's Word, etc. All of a sudden the heavens open up to us and we can see and understand spiritual truths that have not previously been revealed to us.

While "in the Spirit," John saw the throne room of God in Heaven. He had a glimpse of the blazing glory and dazzling beauty of the

Almighty sitting on His throne. God's throne was far more spectacular than that of any Roman emperor. John described the power of God using natural phenomena we can understand such as lightnings, thunders, loud voices, fire, precious stones, and a rainbow. Wow! What an awesome scene of an awesome God.

John saw all of Heaven worshiping God, including 24 elders, a representative number of God's people who overcome the world by the blood of the Lamb and the word of their testimony (see Rev. 12:11). He used "otherworldly" language to describe powerful angels who worship God day and night. They give glory to God as the Creator and sustainer of all things.

The Son of Man, through the pen of John, wanted His persecuted followers to understand that the Lord God Almighty is sovereign over all of His creation. He alone is to be feared and obeyed. He alone is to be worshiped. The vanity and splendor of the imperial cult worship was nothing compared to the majestic greatness of God. God's people should resist "fixing their sandals" before the emperor. God has something much better for them in Heaven.

As John's spiritual eyes were further opened, he saw God holding something in His right hand. He describes what he saw in the following chapter. Let's join John now as he shares his revelation of the Redeemer of mankind.

THE LAMB AND THE SEVEN-SEALED SCROLL (REVELATION CHAPTER 5)

In this chapter, John continues to describe his apocalyptic vision of Heaven. So this is a heavenly scene in which John sees with spiritual eyes the true identity of the real Emperor and Lord and King of the nations. It is not Caesar, nor is it any of the arrogant, prideful leaders of our world today. It is none other than the Lamb of God who is also the

Lion of the Tribe of Judah. May the Spirit of God open our eyes with John to see this reality for ourselves. Amen!

The Lamb and the Scroll (verses 1-7)

As John looks closer, he sees the Almighty God, Creator of the universe, holding a scroll in His right hand. The scroll is written inside and on the back and is sealed with seven seals. What is this seven-sealed scroll and why does God have it in His right hand?

In the Bible, the right hand is the symbol of power and authority. For example, Psalm 98 is a song of victory and praise to God for His salvation and judgment. It begins with this exuberant praise:

> *Oh, sing to the LORD a new song! For He has done marvelous things; His right hand and His holy arm have gained Him the victory* (Psalm 98:1).

The Lord gives the following word of assurance to His people:

> *Fear not, for I am with you; be not dismayed, for I am your God. I will strengthen you, yes, I will help you, I will uphold you with My righteous right hand* (Isaiah 41:10).

The fact that God has this scroll in His right hand is John's way of symbolically saying that God Himself wrote the contents of the scroll. As the Creator of the universe, He can give the scroll to whomever He pleases. As we will see, the scroll contains God's final word of judgment on the nations, but redemption for His people.

In ancient times, people wrote on parchment and scrolls. In our study of God's prophetic message to the believers at Pergamos, we learned that parchment was first developed at Pergamos, from which the word *parchment* is derived. Parchment was made from animal skins, particularly the skins of sheep and goats. We learn in the apostle Paul's letter to Timothy that he made use of parchment (see 2 Tim. 4:13).

Scrolls were primarily written on papyrus which was a paper-like material made from reeds from the Nile delta in Egypt. The books Paul mentioned to Timothy were probably papyrus scrolls. We learn in the Hebrew Bible that the prophets often wrote their messages and visions on a scroll (see Jer. 36; Ezek. 2; Isa. 29; Dan. 12).

Because of the way that papyrus material was made, it was easier for people to write only on one side of the scroll. When it was necessary, they went to the extra trouble to write on both sides. For example, when God gave His words to Ezekiel, He had written on both sides of the scroll. Ezekiel writes:

> Now when I looked, there was a hand stretched out to me, and behold, a scroll of a book was in it. Then He spread it before me; and there was writing on the inside and on the outside, and written on it were lamentations and mourning and woe (Ezekiel 2:9-10).

From this statement we learn that the scroll in Revelation was not the first time that God had written an important message on a scroll.

If the contents of a scroll were to be read only by an authorized person, the writer would seal the scroll to keep its contents private. Only the authorized person could loose the seals and open the scroll. We see an example of this in Isaiah which reads:

> The whole vision has become to you like the words of a book [scroll] that is sealed, which men deliver to one who is literate, saying, "Read this, please;" and he says, "I cannot, for it is sealed" (Isaiah 29:11).

When Daniel was struggling to understand his prophetic vision, the Lord sent an angel to explain its meaning to him. The angel said to Daniel:

> *Now I have come to make you understand what will happen to your people in the latter days, for the vision refers to many days yet to come* (Daniel 10:14).

Then the angel said:

> *But you, Daniel, shut up the words, and seal the book until the time of the end; many shall run to and fro, and knowledge shall increase* (Daniel 12:4).

The angel repeated himself to Daniel:

> *And he said, "Go your way, Daniel, for the words are closed up and sealed till the time of the end"* (Daniel 12:9).

Whenever a scroll was sealed, people knew that the document had not been opened and that the contents written in the document had been kept confidential. Only the authorized person could loose the seals, open the document and read the contents.

The scroll in God's hand is sealed with seven seals. In the Bible, seven is the number of completion or fulfillment. The seven-sealed scroll contains information that represents God's completed or final prophetic word for mankind. I have no doubt in my own mind that this seven-sealed scroll contains the prophetic word of the Lord given to Daniel and sealed until the time of the end. It is God's Word telling us what will happen in the end times.

We all want to know the future, and the contents of the seven-sealed scroll have that information. But it is sealed seven times. Neither John nor us will know God's prophetic word unless someone God has authorized can loose the seals, open the scroll, and read the contents.

As John looked at the scroll, and all of Heaven waited for the seals to be broken, a powerful angel shouted with a loud voice, *"Who is worthy to open the scroll and loose its seals?"* (Rev. 5:2). When John says the angel shouted with a loud voice he wants us to understand that the question resounded throughout all of God's creation from the beginning of time. The voice of the angel calling for an authorized person to loose the seals filled Heaven and Earth. We are not told the name of the angel. Because of the connection to Daniel's vision, it is most likely the same angel that told Daniel to seal the book until the time of the end. Now the angel is saying it is time to open the seals.

All of God's creation in Heaven, on the earth, and in the underworld of the dead, heard the question. This is the question of all questions. It is the most important question that could be asked and it is the most dramatic moment of John's vision. I don't know how long it took for the answer, but no one came forth to claim the right to open the scroll. Not one of God's creatures, angelic or human, no matter how much earthly glory, riches, and power they acquired, was able to come forth and take the scroll from God's hand. Neither the highest archangel nor the most exalted human could take the scroll.

Adam and Eve were there. God created them perfect and put them in a perfect environment but they were disobedient. So they couldn't take the scroll. Abraham was there. He was a great man of faith except when it came to trusting God to give him a son. He couldn't take the scroll. Noah was there, but he had too much wine. He couldn't take the scroll. Moses was there, but he struck the rock. He couldn't take the scroll. Aaron was there, but he made a golden calf. He couldn't take the scroll. King David was there, but he sinned with Bathsheba. He couldn't take the scroll. All of the Hebrew prophets were there, but they didn't fully understand their own prophecies. So they couldn't take the scroll. The disciples of Jesus were there, but they all left Him when He was being tried. They couldn't take the scroll. All the holy saints of God throughout history were there, but all have sinned and come short of the glory of God (see Rom. 3:23). They couldn't take the scroll.

When John realized that not one of God's created beings was authorized to loose the seals, he began to weep bitterly. Unless an authorized person could be found, the contents of the scroll would be kept secret and neither John, nor us, would know the future. Furthermore, God's prophetic word would not go forth which means that evil would continue unabated. There would be no hope for the future. Caesar would prevail.

But at his moment of deepest despair, one of the elders approached John and comforted him with these words:

> *...Do not weep. Behold the Lion of the tribe of Judah, the Root of David, has prevailed to open the scroll and to loose its seven seals* (Revelation 5:5).

Seasoned believers know that "The Lion of the Tribe of Judah" is a term for the Messiah. He is a descendant of Judah who would not only rule as King of the Jews but also as King of kings over the nations.

When Jacob prophesied over his sons, he said that Judah would be the tribe to provide the kings of Israel. Jacob spoke these words over his son:

> *Judah, you are he whom your brothers shall praise; your hand shall be on the neck of your enemies; your father's children shall bow down before you. Judah is a lion's whelp* [cub]; *from the prey, my son, you have gone up. He bows down, he lies down as a lion; and as a lion, who shall rouse him? The scepter shall not depart from Judah, nor a lawgiver from between his feet, until Shilo comes; and to him shall be the obedience of the people* (Genesis 49:8-10).

According to the traditional Jewish interpretation, the word *Shilo* means the one to whom it rightfully belongs, or "he whose it is."[1] (See also Ezekiel 21:27.) It is a Messianic title referring to the descendant of Judah who would be the ultimate King-Messiah to whom the people (Judah and all the nations) would give their obedience. When Jacob says that the scepter shall not depart from Judah until Shilo comes, he means that Israel will continue as an independent nation until the King-Messiah is born and presents Himself to the people in the fulfillment of this prophecy.

Students of Bible history know that the Romans took away the rights of the Jewish leadership to rule themselves in the first century of our era. In other words, they lost their national sovereignty. We see this manifested in the time of Jesus when the Jewish authorities had to seek permission from the Romans to put Jesus to death.

Furthermore, in A.D. 70, the Romans destroyed Jerusalem, burned the Temple to the ground, and scattered the Jews among the nations. This means that Shilo had to be living and presenting Himself to the people before A.D. 70. He could not come after this time because of the prophecy regarding the national sovereignty of the Jewish people. The only person who can possibly fulfill this requirement is Jesus of Nazareth. He is the Lion of the Tribe of Judah. The heart cry of the Jewish leaders who rejected Jesus as Messiah was that the scepter had departed from Judah and Shilo had not come. He had come, but the powerful and prideful priestly leaders rejected Him.

John refers to the Lion of the Tribe of Judah as the Root of David. As a Jewish man, John once again takes us back to the Hebrew Bible to speak of this "worthy One." The prophet Isaiah writes:

> *There shall come forth a Rod from the stem of Jesse* [David's father], *and a Branch shall grow out of his roots. The Spirit of the LORD shall rest upon Him, the Spirit of wisdom and understanding, the Spirit of counsel and might, the Spirit of knowledge and of the fear of the LORD* (Isaiah 11:1-2).

Isaiah prophesies that even though the tribe of Judah and the royal line of David will be cut down like a tree chopped down to a stump, a Branch, meaning a descendant, will grow out of the stump. This Branch will be greater than the original tree because the Spirit of God will rest upon Him.

Isaiah goes on to say that this Branch will establish justice and righteousness on the earth, slay the wicked, establish the Messianic Kingdom of God on the earth and give peace and rest to the world. He summarizes his prediction with these words:

> *And in that day there shall be a Root of Jesse, who shall stand as a banner to the people; for the Gentiles shall seek Him, and His resting place shall be glorious* (Isaiah 11:10).

In the Gospel records, Matthew wrote about a dialogue Jesus had with the Pharisees. He wanted them to consider the prophecies about the Messiah. Jesus asked them:

> *"...[What do you think about the Christ [Messiah]? Whose Son is He?" They said to Him, "The Son of David." He said to them, "How then does David in the Spirit call Him, 'Lord,' saying: 'The LORD said to my Lord, "Sit at My right hand, till I make Your enemies Your footstool"'? If David then calls Him 'Lord,' how is He his Son?" And no one was able to answer Him a word, nor from that day on did anyone dare question Him anymore* (Matthew 22:42-46).

Jesus backed them into a corner, and they couldn't answer His question. David's Greater Son was also his Lord. How could this be unless the Greater Son was both before and after David? He was both David's Lord (the Messiah) and David's Son. Jesus spoke of Himself in this way and said, *"I am the Root and the Offspring of David, the Bright and Morning Star"* (Rev. 22:16).

In Revelation 5:5, the elder tells John that the Lion of the tribe of Judah, the Root of David, has "prevailed." This suggests that He overcame something, and as a result, God found Him to be worthy. What did He overcome? Jesus gives us the answer recorded in the Gospel of John. He says:

> *These things I have spoken to you, that in Me you may have peace. In the world you will have tribulation; but be of good cheer, I have overcome the world* (John 16:33).

Hallelujah! Jesus overcame the world, He overcame sin, He overcame satan, and He overcame death. Jesus was the only perfect human being who always did what pleased His heavenly Father. He was obedient even to the point of dying for our sins. But because He had no sin Himself, death and Hades could not hold Him. As a result, He came forth from the dead in resurrection life and power and has now taken His rightful place by His Father in Heaven. This is what the elder had in mind when he said the Lion and the Root of David had prevailed and was therefore worthy to open the scroll and to loose its seven seals.

Now when John looked to see this Lion, meaning the conquering King in power and authority, he didn't see a great ruler; instead he saw a Lamb standing in the midst of God's throne, the four special angelic beings, and the elders.

Of course, John is using a figure of speech. He didn't see a literal Lamb. What he saw was Jesus, the suffering Servant, the crucified Savior, who, like a lamb, gave His life for the sins of mankind. But unlike sacrificial lambs that were dead, Jesus, the Lamb of God, is alive.

When Jesus came the first time, He came to give His life as the innocent substitutionary sacrifice for our sins. This is why John the Baptist introduced Jesus with these words, *"Behold! The Lamb of God who takes away the sin of the world!"* (John 1:29).

Isaiah also spoke of this ministry of Jesus:

> *Surely He has borne our griefs and carried our sorrows; yet we esteemed Him stricken, smitten by God, and afflicted. But He was wounded for our transgressions, He*

was bruised for our iniquities; the chastisement for our peace was upon Him, and by His stripes we are healed. All we like sheep have gone astray; we have turned, every one, to his own way; and the Lord has laid on Him the iniquity of us all.

He was oppressed and He was afflicted, yet He opened not His mouth; He was led as a lamb to the slaughter, and as a sheep before its shearers is silent, so He opened not His mouth. He was taken from prison and from judgment, and who will declare His generation? For He was cut off from the land of the living; for the transgressions of My people He was stricken. And they made His grave with the wicked—but with the rich at His death, because He had done no violence, nor was any deceit in His mouth.

Yet it pleased the Lord to bruise Him; He has put Him to grief. When You make His soul an offering for sin, He shall see His seed, He shall prolong His days, and the pleasure of the Lord shall prosper in His hand. He shall see the labor of His soul, and be satisfied. By His knowledge My righteous Servant shall justify many... (Isaiah 53:4-11).

Because Jesus was perfectly righteous and willingly gave His life for us, God His Father raised Him from the dead and seated Him at His right hand in Heaven. He did not prevail as the Lion, but as the Lamb. Whereas this is the only reference to Jesus as the Lion, He is referenced as the Lamb 29 times in the Book of Revelation. Because Jesus was willing to be the Lamb, God has exalted Him as the Lion who will return to Earth as the Greater Son of David, the King of the Jews, and the King of kings and Lord of lords over the nations.

Using symbolic language, John says this Lamb is not like any other lamb. Jesus, the Lamb of God, has seven horns and seven eyes which

John interprets to mean the seven Spirits of God. Unlike normal lambs which are weak and helpless, the Lamb of God has complete power (the seven horns) and complete knowledge (the seven eyes). He has the Holy Spirit (the seven Spirits of God) which He sends to execute God's will on the earth. As John learns later in the Book of Revelation, this Lamb is coming to the earth as the Lion to judge and make war against all who oppose God's will (see Rev. 19:11).

In what must have been the greatest moment of John's vision, and as all of Heaven held its breath, Jesus did what no angel or human could do. He took the scroll from the right hand of God. This is the act that establishes Jesus as the Savior, Judge, Redeemer, and King of mankind.

This is the moment Daniel saw in his vision and wrote:

> I was watching in the night visions, and behold, One like the Son of Man, coming with clouds of heaven! He came to the Ancient of Days, and they brought Him near before Him. Then to Him was given dominion and glory and a kingdom. That all peoples, nations, and languages should serve Him. His dominion is an everlasting dominion, which shall not pass away, and His kingdom the one which shall not be destroyed (Daniel 7:13-14).

This is the moment Jesus had in mind when He was interrogated by the High Priest. The High Priest put Jesus under oath and said to Him:

> "...tell us if You are the Christ [Messiah], the Son of God!" Jesus said to him, "It is as you said. Nevertheless, I say to you, hereafter you will see the Son of Man sitting at the right hand of the Power, and coming on the clouds of heaven" (Matthew 26:63-64).

Worthy Is the Lamb (verses 8-14)

When Jesus took the scroll, Heaven and Earth began a spontaneous chorus of praise and worship to God and to the Lamb. The sounds of creation singing a new song of redemption filled Heaven and Earth. Nothing Rome or the Caesars could orchestrate could compare to the exaltation John saw and heard. Caesar is dead; Jesus lives!

It began with those nearest the throne. The four powerful angels and the 24 elders started this heavenly worship by bowing before the Lamb. Each had a harp in one hand and a golden bowl of incense in the other. The harp symbolized their praise and worship while the bowl of incense symbolized the prayers of God's people (see Ps. 141:2; 150:3).

John writes:

> *And they sang a new song, saying: "You are worthy to take the scroll, and to open its seals; for You were slain, and have redeemed us to God by Your blood out of every tribe and tongue and people and nation, and have made us kings and priests to our God; and we shall reign on the earth"* (Revelation 5:9-10).

Jesus is worthy because He has redeemed us. In biblical times, God established that a slave could be redeemed or set free by one who was worthy to purchase his freedom. But one had to qualify to be a redeemer.

In biblical times there were five requirements to be a redeemer. First, the person had to be a near kinsman. In other words, he had to be the nearest kin family member. Second, the person had to be willing to redeem the slave. He could not be made to redeem the one in bondage. Third, the person had to be able to redeem the slave. This means there could be no technicalities that would disqualify the person as a redeemer. Fourth, the person had to be a freeman. A slave could not redeem a slave. Fifth, the potential redeemer had to have the money or price required to redeem the slave. Only when these five requirements were met, was one considered a worthy redeemer. This is the story of Ruth and Boaz as recorded in the Book of Ruth, particularly in chapter 4.

Jesus is worthy to take the scroll, open the seals, and redeem us because He alone has met all of the requirements to be a redeemer. Even though we don't like to acknowledge it, we are all subject to sin, satanic temptations, and the fear of death. Christians call this a sin nature. In Hebrew, Jews call it the *yester hara* (evil inclination). Whatever you choose to call it, this is the universal human condition. God's judgment for this condition is separation from Him, what the Bible calls death. We need to be redeemed or set free. But since we are all sinners, there is none among us who can save us. Even God cannot save us from Heaven. According to His own requirements, God would have to become one of us in order to redeem us.

And this is exactly what God did for us. As God in human flesh, Jesus was one of us, a nearest kin member of the human race. He willingly gave His life for us. He could have called for thousands of angels to come and rescue Him (see Matt. 26:53), but He didn't. He was born to die in our place. Jesus was able to redeem us because He was without sin. Therefore, He could take our place as the innocent substitutionary sacrifice for the sins of all mankind. Because Jesus was perfectly righteous, neither sin, satan, nor death had claims on Him. Therefore, He was free to redeem us. And finally, Jesus was able to pay the price for our redemption. That price was His own pure blood which He shed for us.

Peter says it this way:

> *...you were not redeemed with corruptible things, like silver or gold, from your aimless conduct received by tradition from your fathers, but with the precious blood of Christ [Messiah], as of a lamb without blemish and without spot. He indeed was foreordained before the foundation of the world, but was manifest in these last times for*

you who through Him believe in God, who raised Him from the dead and gave Him glory, so that your faith and hope are in God (1 Peter 1:18-21).

Whereas most religions have an ethno-centered focus on one particular group of people, Jesus has made redemption available for "whosoever will." His offer of redemption is not just for a certain people group; it is for everyone who will call upon His name (see Rom. 10:13). He has redeemed us out of every tribe and tongue and people and nation. Hallelujah! This was predicted in the Book of Psalms which tells us:

Oh, sing to the LORD a new song! Sing to the LORD, all the earth. Sing to the LORD, bless His name; Proclaim the good news of His salvation from day to day. Declare His glory among the nations, His wonders among all peoples (Psalm 96:1-3).

The glorious Son of Man has not only redeemed His people, He has also made us His royal priests on the earth. This was God's promise to the Hebrews when He brought them out of Egypt. He said:

"Now therefore, if you will indeed obey My voice and keep My covenant, then you shall be a special treasure to Me above all people; for all the earth is Mine. And you shall be to Me a kingdom of priests and a holy nation." These are the words which you shall speak to the children of Israel (Exodus 19:5-6).

While the Jewish people often failed to keep God's covenant, as do believers today, Jesus was the one Jewish man who perfectly kept the covenant with His Father in Heaven. Jesus is the perfect Jew and the perfect human. Through our identification with Him, believers from all ethnic backgrounds and nations have the promise of ruling with Him both now and at His coming, as His priests and a light to all the nations.

While Christian believers have not replaced the Jewish people in God's eternal covenant, Jesus has brought us into that covenant by redeeming us and making us His own people. As Peter writes:

> *But you are a chosen generation, a royal priesthood, a holy nation, His own special people, that you may proclaim the praises of Him who called you out of darkness into His marvelous light; who once were not a people but are now the people of God, who had not obtained mercy but now have obtained mercy* (1 Peter 2:9-10).

Rome is no more and the Caesars are dead. God is going to judge the nations of our world and all the would-be Caesars of our day. But the people of God will live forever in God's glorious Kingdom on the earth. Therefore, don't "fix your sandals" before the Emperor nor the anti-God governments of our world. They are nothing compared to the exalted Son of Man and the glorious destiny He has for His people.

Now when the angels of Heaven saw and heard the first chorus of worship, they too joined their voices with those nearest the throne. They said with a loud voice, "...*Worthy is the Lamb who was slain to receive power and riches and wisdom, and strength and honor and glory and blessing!*" (Revelation 5:12).

John says the number of the angels shouting their worship to God was ten thousand times ten thousand and thousands of thousands. Wow! Literally, these phrases could be translated as "myriad upon myriad" which means a number too great to count. It is John's way of saying that all the angels of Heaven, too many to count, all at the same time, shouted their praise and worship to the Lamb. We can't imagine such a noise. All of Heaven was filled with angelic shouts to the Lord. It should take our breath away just contemplating this.

Daniel saw this scene in a vision and said:

I watched till thrones were put in place, and the Ancient of Days was seated; His garment was white as snow, and the hair of His head was like pure wool. His throne was a fiery flame, its wheels a burning fire; a fiery stream issued and came forth from before Him. A thousand thousands ministered to Him; ten thousand times ten thousand stood before Him. The court was seated, and the books were opened (Daniel 7:9-10).

When Enoch wrote his apocalyptic vision, he said he saw tens of millions of angels around the throne.[1] Enoch, Daniel and John are all describing the same scene.

In John's vision, the angels shout a sevenfold honor to the Lamb similar to the praise and worship David offered to the God of Israel:

...Blessed are You, LORD God of Israel, our Father, forever and ever. Yours, O LORD, is the greatness, the power and the glory, the victory and the majesty; for all that is in heaven and in earth is Yours; Yours is the kingdom, O LORD, and You are exalted as head over all. Both riches and honor come from You, and You reign over all. In Your hand is power and might; in Your hand it is to make great and to give strength to all (1 Chronicles 29:10-12).

Because Jesus was faithful to His destiny, God the Father has chosen to share His glory with His Son. We can understand this at the human level. Fathers love to honor their children who uphold the family name, or as we would say, "make him proud." Jesus made His Father in Heaven proud. As a result, God has honored His Son who is the faithful witness, the firstborn from the dead, and the ruler over the kings of the earth.

Finally, John hears all of creation join in the glorious praise and worship of God and the Lamb:

...Blessing and honor and glory and power be to Him who sits on the throne, and to the Lamb, forever and ever! (Revelation 5:13).

This is the fulfillment of Paul's words:

Therefore God also has highly exalted Him [Jesus] *and given Him the name which is above every name, that at the name of Jesus every knee should bow, of those in heaven, and of those on earth, and of those under the earth, and that every tongue should confess that Jesus Christ* [Yeshua the Messiah] *is Lord, to the glory of God the Father* (Philippians 2:9-11).

With all of Heaven and Earth giving glory to God, the four special angels and the 24 elders join in the worship:

Then the four living creatures said, "Amen!" And the twenty-four elders fell down and worshiped Him who lives forever and ever (Revelation 5:14).

May we who are called by His name do the same. May we join the heavenly hosts in unfettered praise and worship to our God. May we, the holy, royal priests of God on the earth, continually offer the sacrifice of praise to God, that is, the fruit of our lips giving thanks to His name. Amen!

Review Questions

1. Write a summary of what you have learned in this lesson. Write the summary in clear, concise words as if you were going to present it to another person.

2. Write an explanation of how you can apply what you have learned in this lesson to your life.

3. Share what you have learned with your family, friends, and members of your study group.

Endnotes

1. The Book of Enoch 14:22; www.sacredtexts.com; accessed December 7, 2011.

Chapter 4

Opening the First Six Seals

REVELATION REVIEW

IN Revelation chapters 4 and 5, John described his prophetic vision of Heaven. He used apocalyptic language to describe his vision in which he saw with spiritual eyes the truth of God's sovereign rule and the believer's victory over evil.

While John was not literally raptured to Heaven, a prophetic door was opened to him to see spiritual realities that he could not understand otherwise. God gave John this revelation to give hope and comfort to His people who were being persecuted by an anti-God government.

All the believers could see was an all-powerful emperor and empire forcing its idolatry on them. They seemed hopeless and helpless against the power, the tyranny, and the evil that was overwhelming them. It was frightening. No one could resist. All seemed lost. Did God know of their circumstances? Why was He allowing this? Was He going to help them? Would good triumph over evil? Should they even try to endure? Was their suffering worth the price they were paying? These are questions God's people have always asked in times of intense suffering.

The believers needed this revelation to encourage them to persevere even to the point of being martyred for their faith. God's sovereign rule and their ultimate victory gave them the assurance they so desperately needed.

John saw the throne room of God in all its glory and beauty and splendor. He saw a special class of powerful angels leading all of Heaven in praise and worship to God. He saw 24 elders clothed in white garments, wearing the victor's crown of life, and sitting with God around His throne. These 24 elders represent the persecuted believers in the seven congregations as well as believers of all time. His point in sharing his vision was to contrast the heavenly throne of God to the earthly throne of the emperor and imperial cult worship.

To believers under intense pressure to worship the emperor, the revelation of God sitting on His throne, and of their ultimately being there with Him, was certainly a source of comfort and hope. God was sovereign. He understood their suffering, and in His own appointed time, He would judge the wicked and reward the righteous. God's people who are faithful will rule and reign with Him. They will overcome death and live in God's glorious presence forever. Yes, the price they pay on Earth is worth it. Yes, they will prevail. They will triumph. Don't bow to the anti-God system of Rome. The One True God will soon pour out His judgments on them.

Looking back, we can see that God did judge Rome. Jesus did defeat Caesar and Christianity, although Greco-Romanized, did become the official religion of the Roman Empire and spread throughout the world. The fact that I am able to write this book to a Christian audience 2,000 years later is living proof of the faithfulness of God and the first-century believers. They did not die in vain. They overcame by the blood of the Lamb and the word of their testimony (see Rev. 12:11). They are our brothers and sisters in the faith and we are the fruit of their faithfulness.

John saw God holding the seven-sealed scroll representing unfilled prophecy. No one was able to take the scroll, loose the seals and read the prophecy. Unless someone could be found who was worthy, God's Word would go unfulfilled. Evil would triumph over good. God's people would have died in vain.

John was overwhelmed with sorrow at the realization that none were worthy. Just when it seemed that all was lost, the slain but resurrected Lamb of God did what no one else could do. He took the scroll from His Father's hand. All of Heaven, those on the earth, and those in the underworld of the dead, worshiped God and the Lamb.

Because He is worthy, Jesus has taken His rightful place as the Lion of the Tribe of Judah. He is the exalted Son of Man able to loose the seals. God's prophetic word of judgment on the nations and the ultimate victory of God's people could now be revealed.

In view of this revelation, believers, past, present, and future, should not bow to the anti-God governments of our world. We should not compromise our beliefs but should remain faithful to the Lord in spite of persecution and tribulation. Our God reigns in the heavens and will soon manifest His righteous judgments on the earth.

When Jesus opened the seals, John recorded the scroll's contents for us in the next chapters of the Book of Revelation. As we read these terrible judgments, let not our hearts be troubled. These judgments are not against God's people. They are against the godless world system. God is bringing it to an end. The kingdoms of this world are becoming the Kingdoms of our Lord and of His Messiah (see Rev. 11:15). God has given John the revelation for our understanding. While our faith will be tested, victory is certain. We face the future with faith, not fear; with hope, not despair; and with joyous expectation of the good that God has promised.

Let us sing the song of Moses, the servant of God, and the song of the Lamb:

> *...Great and marvelous are Your works, Lord God Almighty! Just and true are Your ways, O King of the*

saints [nations]! *Who shall not fear You, O Lord, and glorify Your name? For You alone are holy. For all nations shall come and worship before You, for Your judgments have been manifested* (Revelation 15:3-4).

OPENING THE FIRST SIX SEALS
(REVELATION 6)

I don't know how long all of creation gave their praise and worship to the Lord, but when they finally quieted down, Jesus began to open the seals. The seven seals are the first of three seven-part judgments on the earth. The seventh seal opens seven additional trumpet-shofar judgments while the seventh trumpet-shofar opens up the final seven bowl judgments. The description of these three seven-part judgments makes up most of the Book of Revelation which John records in chapters 6-16. (See the suggested outline of the Book of Revelation in Book 1 of this series to review how the book is organized.)

While there are many good books that go into great detail trying to explain the timing of the events in the Book of Revelation, I do not take that approach in this book. While it is good to understand as much as we can about the end-time events, some of the details are just not that clear in the Bible. When we try to understand and explain every detail with our own Greco-Roman worldview, we discover that we sometimes have to put our interpretations into the details. These are often wrong and misleading as we have to force our own meanings on the text. It is best to present the grand sweep of the book, and let God show us the details as we see them unfold before our very eyes. He is the only One who knows how it all fits together.

This is why Jesus Himself gave the best overview of the Book of Revelation; it is recorded in Matthew 24. His disciples were excited to give Jesus a tour of the Temple buildings. Jesus dampened their spirits by telling them that the Temple would be destroyed. The disciples were puzzled and asked Jesus about the end times. Matthew recorded the dialog:

> *Now as He sat on the Mount of Olives, the disciples came to Him privately, saying, "Tell us, when will these things be? And what will be the sign of Your coming, and of the end of the age?"* (Matthew 24:3).

Jesus answered them with a prophetic outline of events leading up to His coming and the end of the age. I have included a rough comparison of passages from Matthew's and Luke's Gospels and the Book of Revelation, below:

The Gospels	Revelation
False Messiahs (Matt. 24:4-5)	False Messiah (6:2)
Wars (Matt. 24:6-7)	Wars (6:3-4)
Famines (Matt. 24:7)	Famines (6:5-6)
Earthquakes (Matt. 24:7)	Earthquakes (6:12)
Pestilence (Luke 21:11)	Pestilence (6:7-8)
Persecution (Matt. 24:9-10)	Persecution (6:9-11)
Celestial Disorders (Matt. 24:29)	Celestial Disorders (6:12-13)
Further Details (Matt 24:11-28)	Further Details (7:1–18:24)
Son of Man Appears (Matt. 24:30-31)	Son of Man Appears (19:11-16)

The First Seal—The Conqueror (verses 1-2)

In Revelation chapter 6, John records what is written on the scroll of the first six seals. Let's now read his words, one seal at a time. With your Bible open alongside this book, read the Bible verses and then the following comments.

What I find most interesting in verse one is the role of Jesus in opening the seals. While He is returning to Earth as the Lion of the Tribe of Judah (the King and Ruler over the nations), He opens the seals as the Lamb. It is His role as the Lamb of God that makes Him authorized and worthy to open the seals and reveal God's judgments on the earth.

When Jesus was first on the earth, satan offered Him all the kingdoms of the world if Jesus would bypass the cross and worship satan. Jesus rebuked satan and said:

> … "Away with you Satan! For it is written, 'You shall worship the LORD your God, and Him only you shall serve'" (Matthew 4:10).

Because Jesus was faithful to His mission to give His life for our sins, God gave Him the kingdoms of this world. Jesus didn't give in to the temptation. Because He was obedient even to the point of dying for us, God has exalted Him to the place of highest honor (see Phil. 2:8-9).

It is the same with God's people today. As the governments of this world become more and more anti-God, we too will be tempted to compromise in order to avoid suffering. May we, like Jesus, resist this temptation. May we have the conviction and courage to put God first in our lives knowing that He will honor us with victory over the enemy. Paul encourages us with these words:

> For I consider that the sufferings of this present time are not worthy to be compared with the glory which shall be revealed in us (Romans 8:18).

And let the people of God say, "Amen!"

In the opening verses of Revelation 6, one of the four special angels calls to John. His voice is so powerful that John says it is like thunder. Wow! Imagine someone's voice being so loud it sounds like thunder. Think about it. When it was time for the citizens of Roman territories to bow down to their emperor, one of the emperor's worship leaders would call the people to worship. I can guarantee you that his voice did not sound like thunder.

The glory and the worship of the Almighty, and those speaking for Him, far surpasses the puny grandeur of emperors. The self-exalting pomp and ceremony of emperor worship cannot compare to the splendor of Heaven. People who have traveled to Europe can see with their own eyes that ancient Rome is in ruins. Yet, we can see in the Book of Revelation that God's city prepared for His people is eternal. The Roman Empire has been relegated to the dust bins of history, but the Kingdom of God is forever. Modern day "would-be Caesars" will fail. Whatever glory they may achieve will be short-lived; but Jesus is Lord forever.

Paul would remind us:

> *For God did not appoint us to wrath, but to obtain salvation through our Lord Jesus Christ* [Yeshua the Messiah], *who died for us, that whether we wake or sleep, we should live together with Him. Therefore comfort each other and edify one another, just as you also are doing* (1 Thessalonians 5:9-11).

This thundering voice calls John to "come and see." This invitation-command to *"Come and see"* (Rev. 6:1) is repeated for seals two, three, and four. By repeating this phrase, John wants us to understand that he really does see the breaking of the seals. He is not making this up; nor is he hallucinating. He is having a real prophetic vision of the coming judgments on the earth. His vision is not only for the believers in the seven congregations but also for believers of all time, including our time. Let us do our best to understand what we are to "Come and see."

The breaking of the first four seals releases what has been referred to as the "Four Horseman of the Apocalypse." While scholars have speculated on what the first-century believers understood these to be, we don't know what they believed. What we do know is that each horse is a different color and the color symbolizes the reality of its judgment on the earth. The prophet Zechariah also had a vision in which he saw colored horses in a different setting from what John saw (see Zech. 1:8-10).

The first rider John sees is on a white horse. A rider on a white horse is the oriental symbol of a conqueror. So the white horse is a symbol of victory. Because Revelation 19 says that Jesus is returning on a white horse, some scholars have taught that this is a symbol of the victory of Jesus over Caesar and Christianity over Rome. However, this does not make sense when considering the results of the actions of this rider, which are revealed in the next seals.

This rider has a bow and a crown, but no arrows. As mentioned previously, the Greek word for "crown" is *stephanos*, a word that indicates a victory crown more than the crown of a sovereign Lord (see Chapter 2). This is not a king, but a political leader. The mention that the bow and the crown are given to him rather than taken by him could suggest that the world powers willingly accept him as their leader. Perhaps with their support and submission, he establishes his authority as a world dictator. This is indicated by John's statement that the rider goes out conquering.

Our best interpretation of this rider and the white horse is that he is the last of the many false messiahs that Jesus warned about who will deceive the nonbelieving world. He may very well be the one known as the antichrist or anti-Messiah who will appear on the scene at the end of days and whose appearing begins the time of tribulation Jesus outlined. Jesus said this would be a time of great lawlessness and deception.

Because our world conditions are so chaotic, it is easy to see that nations would be willing to relinquish their national sovereignty to a charismatic world leader who would promise peace and prosperity. The Bible indicates that there will be a false "world peace" but that it is a deception (see Ezek. 13:10; Jer. 6:14; 8:11).

It is a false promise which will only lead to war, famine, disease, and suffering on a scale the world has never known. This is made clear in the opening of the next seals. The apostle Paul wrote these words:

> *For when they say, "Peace and safety!" then sudden destruction comes upon them, as labor pains upon a pregnant woman. And they shall not escape* (1 Thessalonians 5:3).

Because world leaders will reject the rule of the One True God, the Lord will allow them to believe and accept the lying deceptions of a false messiah. That is a just judgment. If people will not accept truth, they will believe a lie. While this false messiah will establish his will and a false peace for a short time, the real Messiah, the glorified Son of Man, will destroy him at His coming, as recorded in Revelation 19:11-21.

It is possible that the rider of this white horse is the "Beast From the Sea" described in Revelation 13:1-10. He could be the political leader of the New World Order that the globalist organizations of our day want to establish. Since the United States is the last great superpower, the globalist leaders have worked behind the scenes for decades to weaken the sovereignty of America so it will join the New World Order League of Nations. We would have to be blind not to see this happening before our very eyes. To dismiss this as the rantings of conspiracy theory kooks is to live in denial. It is certainly possible that America will soon become a third-world country.

The three most powerful globalist organizations are the Bilderbergers, the Trilateral Commission, and the Council on Foreign Relations. Their members make up most of the elite of American leaders in politics, the media, education, and banking and finance. With America's financial institutions failing, they believe they are on the verge of achieving their goal. They may be right. For an in-depth explanation of how this subject relates to Bible prophecy and current events, I urge you to read my book entitled *The End of All Things Is at Hand: Are You Ready?* (You can order it from my online bookstore.)

The apostle Paul calls this false messiah *"the lawless one"* who is empowered by satan to deceive the people of world:

> *And then the lawless one will be revealed, whom the Lord will consume with the breath of His mouth and destroy with the brightness of His coming. The coming of the lawless one is according to the working of Satan, with all power, signs, and lying wonders, and with all unrighteous deception among those who perish, because they did not receive the love of the truth, that they might be saved. And for this reason God will send them strong delusion, that they should believe the lie, that they all may be condemned who did not believe the truth but had pleasure in unrighteousness* (2 Thessalonians 2:8-12).

The Second Seal—War (verses 3-4)

When the exalted Lamb of God opens the second seal, the second powerful angel, or living creature, beckons John to *"Come and see."* This time, John sees a fiery red horse. John says three things about the rider of this horse: he takes peace from the earth, he causes people to kill one another, and he is given a great sword. From this we understand that the red horse is the symbol for war.

Jesus said there would be wars and rumors of wars and that nations and kingdoms would fight each other. While His prediction has certainly proven true in history, the rider of this horse will cause wars in the last days that will escalate into a worldwide war and the final Battle of Armageddon. Only the coming of the Lord in Revelation 19 will end the carnage. In His prophetic outline, Jesus said that unless those days are shortened, no one would survive (see Matt. 24:22).

Why do the nations war among themselves? There are three basic reasons. First is the evil in men's hearts to want to rule over themselves apart from God. Psalm 2 reads:

> *Why do the nations rage, and the people plot a vain thing? The kings of the earth set themselves, and the rulers take counsel together, against the LORD and against His Anointed, saying, "Let us break Their bonds in pieces and cast away Their cords from us." He who sits in the heavens shall laugh; the Lord shall hold them in derision. Then He shall speak to them in His wrath, and distress them in His deep displeasure: "Yet I have set My King on My holy hill of Zion"* (Psalm 2:1-6).

The second reason is the evil in men's heart to want to conquer their neighbors. God has appointed boundaries for the nations as we learn in Deuteronomy:

> *When the Most High divided their inheritance to the nations, when He separated the sons of Adam, He set the boundaries of the peoples according to the number of the children of Israel* (Deuteronomy 32:8).

How interesting that God set the boundaries of the nations in relationship to the covenant land He promised to the descendants of Abraham, Isaac, and Jacob. When nations seek to expand their borders beyond what God has allotted to them, wars are the result.

The third reason for wars, which specifically relates to the red horse and the Book of Revelation, is the nations' desire to destroy the reborn state of Israel. One of the major themes of the Bible is that God will bring the Jewish people back to their ancient land in the endtimes in

fulfillment of prophecy. Of the many Scriptures that speak of this subject, probably the most famous is the Valley of Dry Bones in the Book
of Ezekiel:

> *Then say to them, "Thus says the Lord GOD: 'Surely I will
> take the children of Israel from among the nations, wher-
> ever they have gone, and will gather them from every side
> and bring them into their own land'"* (Ezekiel 37:21).

The anti-Semitic leaders of our world hate God, hate the Jews, and
hate Israel. They also hate Bible-believing Christians. They constantly
make their anti-Israel resolutions through the hate-filled, Arab-dom-
inated United Nations. I believe this demon-inspired animosity will
eventually cause a series of wars culminating in Armageddon.

The next war between the Arabs and Israel may not be contained to
the Middle East. It may bring all the nations into the war. Ezekiel writes
about a confederation of nations coming from the north (north of Jerusalem) in the latter days to attack Israel (see Ezekiel 38-39.) The writer
of Psalm 83 tells about an Arab confederacy that seeks, in current-day
verbiage, to "wipe Israel off the face of the earth."

While previous Arab dictators care nothing about their people, they
have kept radical groups in check. But with the leadership changes taking place in Arab countries, it is most likely that radical Islamic groups
such as the Muslim Brotherhood will come to power. They do not recognize the legitimacy of Israel and will do everything they can to fight
Israel. Ironically, the U.S. government is naively recognizing the legitimacy of the Muslim Brotherhood. This will further bring God's judgment on America.

Furthermore, immense gas fields have been discovered in the Medi-
terranean off the coast of Haifa. It is estimated that there is enough gas
for Israel to become completely self-sufficient and a major exporter of
gas for decades. It is also believed that there are huge oil fields located
beneath the gas fields. God is blessing Israel with these natural resources

because the time to favor Zion has come (see Psalm 102). However, all these discoveries will certainly tempt Israel's enemies to attack Israel so they can get the wealth for themselves. This is all written in the Bible.

Zechariah tells us that all the nations will gather to fight against Jerusalem: *"For I will gather all the nations to battle against Jerusalem..."* (Zech. 14:2).

Zechariah further explains Israel's eventual plight:

> *Behold, I will make Jerusalem a cup of drunkenness* [reeling] *to all the surrounding peoples, when they lay siege against Judah and Jerusalem. And it shall happen in that day that I will make Jerusalem a very heavy stone for all peoples; all who would heave it away will surely be cut in pieces, though all nations of the earth are gathered against it* (Zechariah 12:2-3).

The Third Seal—Famine (verses 5-6)

When the exalted Son of Man, the Lamb of God, opens the third seal, the third powerful angel, or living creature, also beckons John to *"Come and see."* This time, John sees a black horse. The rider has a pair of scales in his hand with which he measures wheat and barley for payment. The rider is told not to disturb the oil and the wine. From this description, we understand that the black horse probably symbolizes hyperinflation and famine which are the natural results of war.

In ancient times, when merchants wanted to sell their products, they brought them in bulk to the *shuk*, the outdoor marketplace. The *shuk* is much like a farmers' market today. Instead of nice fancy packaging marked with the price, the merchant offered his grains and herbs and spices and other dry goods such as nuts, dates, figs, etc., loose in bins. If you wanted to know how much the merchant was selling his product for, he would weigh the product in his scale with the produce in one balance and a weight in the other. He would then tell you how much you would have to pay to buy the produce.

Our modern day *shuks* (grocery stores) have their own hi-tech version of this ancient form of buying and selling. Stores assign numbers to different produce items. Customers then select these items, place them on the store scale, and punch in the assigned numbers. The computer compares the weight of the produce to the price and prints out a price sticker. The sticker saves time during checkout because the price is already on the bag.

John was writing to people who were used to this type of marketplace buying and selling (with the exception of the computer). He heard a voice from among the four living creatures calling out the price of the produce. In the vision, the produce items were bread and oil and wine. These were the staples of people living in Bible times. The vision revealed that they were going to have to pay a lot more than normal for their basic, everyday food items.

Wheat was considered a better grain than barley so it was more expensive. When John received this revelation, a denarius was a Roman silver coin about the size of a dime that was equal to a day's wage. The shopper would have to pay a denarius just to buy one quart of wheat which was the amount of bread a person would consume in one meal. He could buy three quarts of barley for a denarius which would enable him to have three meals for the day.

This means that the shopper would have to work all day just to buy enough bread for one person. It did not cover the wife and kids. This price was ten to fifteen times the normal price of the produce. That meant working all day just to buy a loaf of bread and nothing else—no oil and no wine. The economic condition in which prices exceed the value of the product is called *hyperinflation*.

Simply put, hyperinflation is caused when the government prints an excessive supply of money without a comparable increase in goods and services. This results in an imbalance in the supply and demand for money. As the government prints more money, it has less value (purchasing power). It doesn't take long before other governments and the citizens lose confidence in the currency. The government panics and prints more money which means it takes even more to purchase the same goods and services. Then at a certain point, the currency becomes worthless.

To give you some examples of how bad this can be, in Germany in 1923 the highest monthly inflation rate was 29,500 percent. This amounted to a daily inflation of 20.9 percent. Prices doubled in 3.7 days. In Hungary in 1946, the highest daily rate of inflation was 207 percent. Prices doubled every 15 hours. In Zimbabwe in 2008, the highest daily inflation rate was 98 percent. Prices doubled in 24.7 hours. This information is readily available by researching articles on the impact hyperinflation has on nations.

If the United States government continues to print money with no comparable increase in goods and services, this could easily cause a massive devaluation of the U.S. dollar and a further weakening of the U.S. economy. This could cause other governments to lose confidence in the dollar as the currency of choice. If this monetary policy is coupled with war, it could certainly create hyperinflation.

Think about what you would have to pay for basic food items if the price doubled each day. On Monday the price for a loaf of bread might be $3.00. On Tuesday it would be $6.00. By Sunday, the price of a loaf of bread would be $192.00. This is more than a day's wage for most folks. This is a very real possibility for the U.S.

In addition to hyperinflation, the U.S. could easily experience a severe economic depression. This is the opposite of hyperinflation. In a time of economic depression, prices go down. While it might seem good to see prices go down, in an economic depression they go down in an out-of-control spiral as sharp as the upward movement seen in hyperinflation. Since people anticipate that prices will go down, they postpone buying until the prices are lower. The result is that companies are not able to sell their products and services at a profit. When companies are not able to sell their products and services at a profit, they stop buying from their vendors, curtail their business operations, and terminate employees. Even though prices for goods and services are lower, few people can buy anything because most don't have jobs.

The worst case scenario is what economists call *stagflation*. Stagflation is the perfect economic storm. This situation combines the worse features of inflation and depression. In this situation, prices for goods and services continue to rise even as economic depression causes millions of people to lose their jobs. As God continues to judge American materialism and greed, the U.S. will certainly experience some measure of hyperinflation, depression, and stagflation. The wealth of the middle class will be completely destroyed. Only God's people who have been obedient to Him and good stewards of His resources will survive the economic catastrophe that I believe is coming to America. Those who have ears, let them hear!

The Fourth Seal—Disease and Death (verses 7-8)

When Jesus opened the fourth seal, the fourth living creature called out to John to *"Come and see."* This time John saw a pale horse. The general interpretation is that the color is a ghastly pale green. John learns that the name of the rider of this horse is *Death* and *Hades*. Since death represents the physical grave and Hades the abode of dead souls, they are considered one and the same. John hears the unthinkable: that Death and Hades were given power over a fourth of the population of the earth to kill with sword, with hunger, with death, and by the beasts of the earth.

In the Hebrew Bible, we learn that the Lord pronounced similar judgments when His people continued to reject Him. The Lord spoke through Ezekiel and said that even if Noah, Daniel, and Job were there, He would not spare His judgment on the people. But God also said He would leave a remnant who would survive and turn to Him. (See Ezekiel 14:12-22.)

The natural results of war and famine are plagues, disease, and death. Tragically, throughout history, whenever there have been major wars, people suffered in these ways. Many who survived the wars died of building collapses, fires, floods, starvation, crowded living conditions, poor sanitation, contaminated water supplies, exposure to the elements, and the spreading of diseases such as typhoid and cholera.

Now that we have weapons of mass destruction, it is easy to understand how nuclear weapons, along with biological and chemical warfare, could destroy a fourth of the population of the earth. With a world population of close to 7 billion people, this would mean more than 1.5 billion people would die when the fourth seal is opened. With such a monumental tragedy, we can also understand how wild animals would attack weak and sickly human beings. Yet, even with such terrible destruction, God would bring three-fourths of the world's population through this judgment and give them time to repent.

As we read about these terrible judgments coming on the earth, we wonder how a loving God could cause such suffering. The answer is that God does not cause this suffering. Mankind causes this due to the hardness of his heart. It is the result of the evil in people's hearts to live their lives without God. While God is longsuffering with us, there does come a point when God knows that we are not going to turn from our sins and seek Him. Since the masses of people do not want Him, God removes His covering of protection and provision and leaves mankind to himself. While God cares for His own people, those who reject Him end up destroying themselves which we see in the opening of these seals. So please, let's not blame God for our own failings.

The Fifth Seal—The Cry of the Martyrs (verses 9-11)

When Jesus opens the fifth seal, none of the four living creatures call John to "Come and see." Whereas the first four seals related to judgments on the earth which needed to be revealed to John, the fifth seal is a heavenly scene. Since John is having a prophetic vision of what is taking place in Heaven, it is not necessary to call him forth. He can see this for himself. And what he sees is certainly heartbreaking.

John sees under the altar in Heaven the souls of those who have been martyred for the Word of God and their testimony. Obviously this is not a time of "easy-believism." There will not be any casual believers during this time on the earth. There won't be any "Sunday-morning Christians" who live for themselves the rest of the week. There will not be any "mega churches." Like the believers in the seven congregations of the first century, the people of God will be persecuted and scattered, and many will be martyred. This situation will certainly distinguish true believers from those who profess faith but don't really possess faith.

In John's vision, these martyrs are crying out for justice. They want to know how long they have to wait before God avenges them. The Lord comforts them by clothing them with white robes, but tells them they have to wait a little longer until His mercy has been satisfied. Then He will judge the wicked. Unfortunately, more would be martyred for their faith. It is very important for us to understand that God's further judgments described in the Book of Revelation are His answer to the prayers of these faithful believers. Please remember this as we read about these horrific events in John's Revelation.

Anyone who tries to live a godly life in this world can certainly understand the heart cry of these martyrs. The Lord's people often groan to themselves and to the Lord for His soon return to put an end to the evil in our world. It is a normal and natural desire for godly people to grow weary of evil and long for righteousness. We too ask the question, "Lord how much longer are You going to put up with the evil in our world? How much longer will it be before You judge the wicked?"

John says that he sees these souls under the altar. This does not necessarily mean that he saw a literal altar but that he saw the altar in his vision. In ancient times, people built altars to their gods and made sacrifices to them. They did this to appease the anger of their gods. This is because the life of the flesh is in the blood. They hoped their gods would accept the blood of the animal in their place. When making the sacrifices, they would pour out the blood of the animal under the altar.

The Lord also required His people to make sacrifices, but with a major difference. One of the Hebrew words translated "offering" is *korban*. The word means to "draw near." In other words, the people were instructed to offer sacrifices to God as a means to draw near to Him, not to appease His wrath. God provided the system of the blood of the innocent substitutionary sacrifice that stood in place of the people. This was the way God could judge sin while showing mercy to the sinner. These souls were described as being under the altar because they chose to draw near to God rather than the anti-God world system.

At the Temple in Jerusalem, the blood of the sacrifices was poured into a basin underneath the altar. Water then carried the blood from the Temple Mount to the Kidron Valley. When the people saw the blood and water, they knew the Lord had accepted their sacrifices. Likewise, the blood of these martyrs was an acceptable sacrifice to the Lord. They had not died in vain.

John says that these souls are given white robes. We learned previously that white in the Bible and in pagan religious services past and present is a symbol of purity. The psalmist wrote:

> *Who may ascend into the hill of the LORD? Or who may stand in His holy place? He who has clean hands and a pure heart...* (Psalm 24:3-4).

Jesus said, *"Blessed are the pure in heart for they shall see God"* (Matt. 5:8). He also promised those who overcome that they would be given white garments (see Rev. 3:5). These believers are given white robes and are in the presence of God because they were spiritually and morally pure.

There is an interesting theological question regarding these souls and their white robes. Once again, we don't know whether John meant that they were literally given white robes or whether this was his apocalyptic way of saying they were in the presence of God because of their pure lives on the earth. If we are to understand this literally, then these believers are given real white robes to clothe their naked souls until they receive new resurrected bodies. While we don't know all the theological answers, we do know that these believers overcame the world and entered the presence of God. And that is what is important.

The Sixth Seal—Cosmic Changes (verses 12-17)

In the sixth seal, John sees major upheaval taking place in Heaven which in turn causes cataclysmic changes on the earth. This is an apocalyptic way of saying that God is now pouring out His wrath on the earth with such power and force that all of Heaven and Earth are being shaken. Since this is apocalyptic symbolism, we would not necessarily interpret these events literally (although we may do so); instead, we could simply realize that God's holy wrath is about to be manifested on the earth.

This is not to say that we should deny the possibility that the Lord might bring about these cataclysmic changes in a literal sense. The challenge is for John to be able to explain what he sees in human language. Furthermore, our human minds simply cannot grasp the magnitude of such events. However this happens, the physical world as we know it is going to change beyond what we can comprehend. God will be creating a new Heaven and a new Earth (see Rev. 21:1).

John's description of these cosmic disturbances is not new. We find similar descriptions in the Hebrew Bible connected with *the Day of the Lord.* This is the phrase used by the prophets to speak of the outpouring of God's wrath against evil at the end of days. They described the response of the people of the world in terms similar to John's statement that the haters of God would try to hide from Him.

Isaiah wrote that, in the Day of the Lord, His enemies will crawl with fear into holes in the ground (see Isa. 2:10-21). The heavens will turn black and neither the stars, nor the moon, nor the sun will give their light (see Isa. 13:10). Isaiah also said that the heavens will melt away and disappear like a rolled-up scroll and the stars will fall from the sky (see Isa. 34:4).

In their apocalyptic visions, Jeremiah and Ezekiel said the heavens will become dark so that the sun, the moon, and the stars do not give out their light (see Jer. 4:23,28; Ezek. 32:7-8). In Hosea's vision of the Day of the Lord, he said the people will beg the mountains to bury them and the hills to fall on them (see Hos. 10:8).

Joel said this would be such a terrible time of God's judgment that the cry would be, *"Who can endure it?"* (Joel 2:11). Joel also wrote that the sun and moon and the stars will be darkened (see Joel 2:31; 3:15).

Nahum wrote that the awesome manifestation of the holy wrath of the Lord would cause the mountains to quake and crumble to dust, the hills to melt, and the earth to tremble (earthquakes). He too asked the question of who could survive the fierce anger of the Day of the Lord (see Nah. 1:5-6).

Zephaniah gave one of the most terrifying descriptions of the Day of the Lord. He called it a day of terrible distress and anguish. He said it would be a day of ruin and desolation, a day of darkness and gloom, of clouds, blackness, trumpet calls, and battle cries. He added that the Lord would make a terrifying end of all the people on the earth (see Zeph. 1:14-18). Malachi also asked the question of who would be able to endure the Day of the Lord (see Mal. 3:2).

In His summary of the end times, Jesus gave a similar description of these cosmic changes. He said:

> *Immediately after the tribulation of those days the sun will be darkened, and the moon will not give its light; the stars will fall from heaven, and the powers of the heavens will*

be shaken. Then the sign of the Son of Man will appear in heaven, and then all the tribes of the earth will mourn, and they will see the Son of Man coming on the clouds of heaven with power and great glory. And He will send His angels with a great sound of a trumpet [shofar], and they will gather together His elect from the four winds, from one end of heaven to the other (Matthew 24:29-31).

Jesus added: *"Heaven and earth will pass away, but My words will by no means pass away"* (Matt. 24:35).

Here is one final word, this time from Peter:

But the day of the Lord will come as a thief in the night, in which the heavens will pass away with a great noise, and the elements will melt with fervent heat; both the earth and the works that are in it will be burned up. Therefore, since all these things will be dissolved, what manner of persons ought you to be in holy conduct and godliness, looking for and hastening the coming of the day of God, because of which the heavens will be dissolved, being on fire, and the elements will melt with fervent heat? Nevertheless we, according to His promise, look for new heavens and a new earth in which righteousness dwells (2 Peter 3:10-13).

Wow! Just writing these words leaves me breathless. No wonder the haters of God hide in caves and beg the mountains and rocks to fall on them. They cannot face the judgments of God and of the Lamb on this terrible and great Day of the Lord. We can see that being martyred for the Lord is much better than being the object of His wrath. Let the people of God say, "Amen!"

REVIEW QUESTIONS

1. Write a summary of what you have learned in this lesson. Write the summary in clear, concise words as if you were going to present it to another person.

2. Write an explanation of how you can apply what you have learned in this lesson to your life.

3. Share what you have learned with your family, friends, and members of your study group.

Chapter 5

God's Seal of Protection

WE learned in the previous chapter that the exalted Son of Man, Jesus the Messiah, opened the seven-sealed book that reveals the future. This book contains information about the coming judgments on the earth. To review, the seven seals are the first of three seven-part judgments that God will unleash on the earth against those who oppose Him. The seventh seal opens seven additional trumpet-shofar judgments while the seventh trumpet-shofar opens the final seven bowl judgments. These judgments are not against God's people but reveal the divine justice of a holy God against those who oppose Him. Although most see this as a time of doom and gloom, the judgments are actually God's answer to the prayers of the saints who were martyred for their faith.

While God is love, His love is not an emotional sentimentalism as is human love. God always extends His holy love to us, but ultimately His mercy is only imparted to those who will receive it. God is long-suffering and not willing that any should perish. But for those who resist Him, God's only choice is to administer His justice. God is always extending His mercy to us. But if we harden our hearts against Him, He must administer His just judgments.

God's love is what we sometimes call "tough love." It is a holy love. Because we human parents often lack the will to discipline our children, we sometimes facilitate our children's irresponsible behavior. This means we can make the situation worse rather than better. When we eventually realize that our kindness is not helping our children, we take a "tough love" approach. If we are honest with ourselves, we certainly know that God must do the same with us. He must act. Any parent should be able to understand God's dealings with rebellious children.

We see this in the story of Moses and Pharaoh in the Book of Exodus. The Lord sent Moses to Pharaoh with the message to let His people go from Egypt. Through these warnings, God gave Pharaoh every opportunity to obey the Word of the Lord. In this way, God was extending His mercy to Pharaoh. Each time Pharaoh refused, the Lord sent a plague as a judgment.

As we know, the Lord sent ten plagues to soften Pharaoh's heart. These were ten opportunities for Pharaoh to receive God's mercy. But each time Pharaoh hardened his heart. When it was clear to all that Pharaoh would not receive God's mercy, there was no point in God continuing to offer it to him. So when God did administer His final judgment, His judgment was just.

Don't we do this ourselves? We may extend repeated kindnesses to others hoping they will respond. But eventually, when we realize they are not going to respond, there is no sense in our continuing to help them. We give them up to their own ways. This does not mean that we don't love them; it means there is no further point in trying to help them.

It is always God's first choice to impart His mercy. His heart grieves for all of us when we go astray. But if we will not receive His mercy, we will experience His judgments. As we see God administer His judgments in the Book of Revelation, please, let us not blame God for the suffering His judgments bring to the unrighteous. While human beings normally blame God for their suffering, more often than not, humans bring His judgments upon themselves. And, as I said, these judgments are God's answer to the prayers of His people for justice.

GOD'S SEAL OF PROTECTION
(REVELATION 7)

When the prophet Habakkuk learned of the coming judgments of the Lord in his day, his prayer was *"O Lord…in wrath remember mercy"* (Hab. 3:2). This should be the prayer of believers for the challenging days ahead.

Chapter seven in the Book of Revelation gives us an example of how God does remember mercy by putting a seal of protection on His own before administering further judgments on the unrighteous. As we read the rest of the Book of Revelation, may we flee to Him for His mercy rather than curse Him for His wrath.

Impending Judgment (verse 1)

Chapter 7 is divided into two parts. The first eight verses inform us about the sealing of God's people before His further judgments. In verses 9-17 we learn about a great multitude of believers who are alive during the time of the Great Tribulation that is coming to the earth. John sees them overcoming and before the throne of God. Let's now study the sealing of God's people.

In the chapter's opening verse, John sees four angels standing at the four corners of the earth holding the four winds of the earth. They are ready to release these four winds which will cause terrible devastation. What are these four winds?

Since John is using apocalyptic language, we cannot be sure whether they are natural winds that God will release or whether they represent demonic forces (or are a combination of both). The result of the angels releasing the four winds is the opening of the seventh seal described in chapter 8. The seventh seal is the seven trumpet-shofar judgments and the seventh trumpet-shofar is the seven bowl judgments. So the seventh seal contains the information about the remaining judgments described in the next chapters in the Book of Revelation.

The prophet Daniel used similar language in his apocalyptic description of the coming days of judgment. The text reads:

> *Daniel spoke, saying, "I saw in my vision by night, and behold, the four winds of heaven were stirring up the Great Sea. And four great beasts came up from the sea, each different from the other"* (Daniel 7:2-3).

The prophet Zechariah saw something similar in his apocalyptic vision recorded in Zechariah 6:1-8. He described four chariots pulled by different colored horses. When Zechariah inquired into the meaning of his vision, an angel told him that the four chariots symbolized four spirits, or winds of Heaven (see Zech. 6:5).

Since John, Daniel, and Zechariah were all writing in an apocalyptic style, the identity of the four winds is not that clear. And that is OK. The Western mind has a tendency to seek knowledge for the sake of knowledge. While it is good to learn, it is not necessary that we understand every detail in the Book of Revelation. We need to be delivered from the "pride of knowledge." What is important is that we are walking with God and are prepared to live overcoming lives in the days ahead.

While we may not clearly know the exact nature of the four winds, what we do know is that releasing them will bring further destruction on the earth. In view of this, the Lord will not allow the four winds to be released until His people are sealed and therefore protected from what is to follow. This is an example of God's mercy during these terrible judgments.

Holding Back Further Judgments (verses 2-3)

Here we see God's mercy in action. He sends an angel to tell the four angels to hold back the four winds of further judgment until God's people are protected. When the Lord opened the sixth seal, the unrighteous of the world hid from God and cried out, *"For the great day of His wrath has come, and who is able to stand?"* (Rev. 6:17). The answer is that the people of God are able to stand because the Lord seals them for protection. Hallelujah!

The Lord knows those who are His just as parents know their own children. In a Scripture we noted earlier, the prophet Nahum writes, *"The LORD is good, a stronghold in the day of trouble; and He knows those who trust in Him"* (Nah. 1:7). The apostle Paul gave the same word of comfort and encouraged God's people to live holy lives. He even referred to God sealing His own. Paul wrote to Timothy:

> *Nevertheless the solid foundation of God stands, having this seal: "The Lord knows those who are His," and, "Let everyone who names the name of Christ* [Messiah] *depart from iniquity"* (2 Timothy 2:19).

We must distinguish God's judgments on the wicked from the wicked persecuting the righteous. While God does not promise to spare His people from persecution and tribulation, there are numerous examples in the Hebrew Bible of God protecting His own before releasing His judgments. We learn in Genesis 6-8 that God saved Noah and his family in the ark before He judged the world with the great flood. He delivered Lot before destroying Sodom and Gomorrah (see Gen. 18-19). In the Exodus story, God did not rapture His people out of Egypt. He protected them and then delivered them once His judgments were over.

In the Book of Ezekiel we learn that God purposed to destroy the wicked in Jerusalem. But first, He instructed an angel to go through the city of Jerusalem and put His mark on the foreheads of His righteous remnant. They were marked for protection just as these are marked. (See Ezekiel 9.) We will discuss this mark later when we study Revelation chapter 14. But for now, let's look more closely at the sealing of the 12 tribes.

Sealing God's People for Protection (verses 4-8)

John describes the sealing of God's people in verses 4 through 8. Being a Jewish believer, he writes that there are 12,000 of God's holy remnant from each of the 12 tribes of Israel making a total of 144,000. It is interesting that satan has his own counterfeit seal during this time. He empowers the False Prophet to put the Mark of the Beast on the forehead or in the right hand of the unrighteous (see Rev. 13:16-18).

Scholars who interpret the Book of Revelation in a more literal sense believe that this is actually 144,000 Jews, and Jews only, who are sealed. Others who interpret the Book of Revelation as apocalyptic literature understand the number to be symbolic of both Jewish believers and believing non-Jews who are grafted in to the Jewish believers. It is certainly not apostate Christianity...

As Western believers, we must understand that Christians are part of the Commonwealth of Israel and have become one new man with them (see Eph. 2:12-22). Speaking symbolically, Jewish believers are not grafted into the Christians' Christmas tree but Christians are grafted into their Olive tree (see Rom. 11.) The Church is not Israel, but is joined with Israel. While Abraham is the natural father of the Jewish people, he is the spiritual father of all true believers (see Gal. 3:28-29). He is "Our Father Abraham."

A natural example of this relationship was when Britain was still Great Britain. Its vast empire covered much of the world. Numerous nations were part of the Commonwealth of Britain. They enjoyed the benefits of being politically related to Britain, but they were not Britain; nor did they replace Britain.

So it is with non-Jewish believers. Christians enjoy the blessings and benefits of the New Covenant through our spiritual relationship with Jesus, our Jewish Lord and Savior. We are joined to Israel, but we are not Israel; nor have we replaced Israel. Christians are called to comfort God's Jewish people and stand with them in the difficult days ahead (see Isa. 40:1).

While it is impossible to say for sure, we should not be dogmatic; it may be that the 144,000 are a representative remnant of Jewish believers, along with non-Jewish believers who were joined to them. Of course, we will have a much clearer understanding as we get closer to the unfolding of these events.

I believe Zechariah saw this "One New Man" company of people when he wrote,

> *Thus says the LORD of hosts; "In those days ten men* [a representative number] *from every language of the nations shall grasp the sleeve* [tzitzit] *of a Jewish man, saying, 'Let us go with you, for we have heard that God is with you' "* (Zechariah 8:23).

Jesus spoke of this company of people in His teaching given in Matthew 25. He explained the judgment of the nations at His coming and used words His listeners could understand. He talked about sheep and goats. Just as a shepherd separates his sheep from his goats, the Lord says He will separate the righteous (the sheep) from the unrighteous (the goats) at His coming.

Jesus told us that the basis of this separation is how the Gentiles treat the Jews during the time of tribulation. Those who help the Jewish people will be considered righteous because their actions are proof of their faith. (See Matthew 25:31-46.) Nonbelievers certainly would not help the Jewish people because they hate the Jews and the God of the Jews, which is why they have accepted the Mark of the Beast.

We already have a 20th-century precedent of this scenario; Christians such as Corrie Ten Boom and many others cared for and protected the Jews from the Nazis during the Holocaust. These believers certainly didn't value their lives to the point of wanting to escape the Nazis at the expense of the Jews.

How can Christians bless, comfort, feed, cloth, visit, and minister to the Jewish people during these dreadful times if Christians escape to Heaven while leaving the Jews behind on the earth to struggle for themselves? What kind of love would that be? Are we so spiritually soft and spoiled that we would leave some of our spiritual family behind to save ourselves? Do we have such little love and care for God's chosen people that we would abandon them? God forgive us.

The Listing of the 12 Tribes

An interesting observation about this listing of the 12 tribes is that it is slightly different from the lists of the 12 tribes mentioned in various places in the Hebrew Bible. In fact, the list of the tribes is found 18 times. For this discussion, we must go all the way back to the Book of Genesis.

One of the most remarkable chapters in the Bible is Genesis 49. This is the chapter that records Jacob's blessing of his 12 sons. Genesis reads:

> *And Jacob called his sons and said, "Gather together, that I may tell you what shall befall you in the last days..."* (Genesis 49:1).

Jacob then pronounced a blessing in the form of a prophecy over each of his sons. Notice he said that the prophecy regards their future "in the last days."

Jacob, now called Israel, spoke a prophetic word of blessing over his sons based on what he perceived by the Spirit to be their character. After blessing his sons, Genesis reads:

> *All these are the twelve tribes of Israel, and this is what their father spoke to them. And he blessed them; he blessed each one according to his own blessing* (Genesis 49:28).

This was Jacob's last act before he died. His final request to his sons was that they would not leave his body in Egypt but would carry it to the land God promised his people and bury him at the cave of Machpelah alongside of Abraham and Sarah, Isaac and Rebekah, and Leah (see Gen. 49:29-33).

The names of the 12 children of Israel and the tribes which came from them are given in the Genesis 49 account. They are:

1. Reuben

2. Simeon

3. Levi

4. Judah

5. Zebulun

6. Issachar

7. Dan

8. Gad

9. Asher

10. Naphtali

11. Joseph (Joseph's sons were Ephraim and Manasseh and are usually listed in place of Joseph)

12. Benjamin

The names of the 12 children of Israel given in Revelation are as follows:

1. Judah

2. Reuben

3. Gad

4. Asher

5. Naphtali

6. Manasseh

7. Simeon

8. Levi

9. Issachar

10. Zebulun

11. Joseph

12. Benjamin

At first glance, we notice that neither Dan nor Ephraim are listed in the Revelation chapter. Joseph, who represented both Ephraim and Manasseh in the Genesis list, is also listed in the Revelation list. However, Manasseh is listed separately in the latter list (which omits Dan). We don't know exactly why Ephraim and Dan are not mentioned in the Revelation list. Some scholars believe it is because of their idolatry.

We learn that early on the tribe of Dan had a problem with idolatry (see Judg. 18). Also, Jeroboam, the rebellious king in the north, set up two golden calves for idol worship in the territory of these tribes. He built shrines to these idols, made sacrifices to them, appointed counterfeit priests, and established counterfeit festivals. In First Kings 12:25-33 we learn that these idol worship centers were set up in Bethel (Ephraim bordering the land allotted to Benjamin) and Dan.

THE TEN LOST TRIBES OF ISRAEL

Just before King David died, he appointed his son, Solomon, to succeed him. Solomon was the wisest man of his time. God blessed him with great riches and honor. His greatest achievement was building the Temple in Jerusalem. But Solomon took many foreign wives who led him into worshiping their gods. In order to support their lifestyle, Solomon oppressed the people with excessive taxes and forced labor. When Solomon died in 930 B.C., the people revolted. There was a civil war which divided the kingdom of Israel between the north and the south.

Bible readers are well-acquainted with this history. To review, the northern kingdom was called Israel and consisted of ten tribes. Its capital was Samaria. The northern kingdom had 19 kings from nine different families. They were all evil and led the people into idol worship.

As we just noted, Jeroboam set up shrines in the northern kingdom and led the people into idolatry. When God saw that they would not repent, He allowed Assyria to conquer them in 721 B.C.:

> *For the children of Israel walked in all the sins of Jeroboam which he did; they did not depart from them, until the LORD removed Israel out of His sight, as He said by all His servants the prophets. So Israel was carried away from their own land to Assyria, as it is to this day* (2 Kings 17:22-23).

The southern kingdom was called Judah and consisted of two tribes, Judah and Benjamin. Jerusalem was its capital. It was conquered by Babylon whose initial siege was in 606 B.C. Babylon finally destroyed Jerusalem in 586 B.C. and took some of the people captive. The southern kingdom had 19 kings and one queen, all from the line of David. Some were good while others were evil.

There were three organized Jewish expeditions of these "southern exiles" from Babylon back to the land. Zerubbabel led the first expedition in the year 536 B.C. We learn that 50,000 Jews accompanied him (see Ezra 2:64-65). Ezra led the second return in 458 B.C. but only 1,750 men plus women and children accompanied him (see Ezra 8). Nehemiah led the last expedition in 445 B.C. (see Neh. 2:1-8).

Because there was no organized return of the northern tribes from Assyria to Israel, they have been referred to as the ten lost tribes of Israel. But does the Bible support this view? While some were definitely deported as the Bible tells us, most Jews in the northern kingdom remained in the north and kept their tribal identity, intermarried with the Assyrians who had been placed in Israel to form the Samaritans, or migrated to Judah in the south.

Those who were deported were never lost—they were scattered and kept by God until the day when He would return them to their ancient land. I personally have met Jews now living in Israel who recently made *aliyah*, meaning they "went up" or returned to Israel, from India. They believe they are descendants of the tribe of Manasseh. I have met Ethiopian Jews who have made *aliyah* and are recognized as the descendants of the tribe of Dan.

While it is interesting to learn different views from historians and scholars, the Bible is our standard of truth. Let's read some Bible verses to substantiate that the ten tribes of Israel were never lost. As we read these verses, please keep an open mind because what the Bible actually says is often different from what we have always been taught and believed.

As just noted, when the kingdom was divided in 930 B.C., Jeroboam set up idol worship in the north. At that time devout Levites and priests in the north refused to participate in the idolatry. They left the north and migrated to Judah in the south:

> *And from all their territories the priests and the Levites who were in all Israel took their stand with him* [Rehoboam in the south]. *For the Levites left their common-lands and their possessions and came to Judah and Jerusalem, for Jeroboam and his sons had rejected them from serving as priests to the Lord* (2 Chronicles 11:13-14).

When these priests and Levites left, Jeroboam replaced them with his own self-appointed priests:

> *Then he* [Jeroboam] *appointed for himself priests for the high places, for the demons, and the calf idols which he had made* (2 Chronicles 11:15).

This open act of idolatry was more than the faithful in the north could take. Many from all the tribes left the north and followed the Levites to the south:

> *And after the Levites left, those from all the tribes of Israel, such as set their heart to seek the LORD God of Israel, came to Jerusalem to sacrifice to the LORD God of their fathers. So they strengthened the kingdom of Judah, and made Rehoboam the son of Solomon strong for three years, because they walked in the way of David and Solomon for three years* (2 Chronicles 11:16-17).

King Asa ruled in Judah from about 910 to 869 B.C. He was a godly king who revived worship of the God of Israel. When the people saw that God was with Asa, they rallied to him in great numbers from both the north and the south:

> *Then he gathered all Judah and Benjamin, and those who dwelt with them from Ephraim, Manasseh, and Simeon, for they came over to him in great numbers from Israel when they saw that the LORD his God was with him....*

Then they entered into a covenant to seek the LORD God of their fathers with all their heart and with all their soul (2 Chronicles 15:9,12).

Hezekiah ruled Judah from 715 to 686 B.C. This was after Assyria conquered the north. According to the Bible, many from the ten tribes were still living in the land. We learn in Second Chronicles 30 that King Hezekiah invited them to Jerusalem to celebrate the Passover:

And Hezekiah sent to all Israel and Judah, and also wrote letters to Ephraim and Manasseh, that they should come to the house of the LORD at Jerusalem, to keep the Passover to the LORD God of Israel....For a multitude of the people, many from Ephraim, Manasseh, Issachar, and Zebulun, had not cleansed themselves, yet they ate the Passover contrary to what was written. But Hezekiah prayed for them, saying, "May the good LORD provide atonement for everyone who prepares his heart to seek God, the LORD God of his fathers, though he is not cleansed according to the purification of the sanctuary" (2 Chronicles 30:1,18-19).

Josiah was a good king who ruled in Judah from 640 to 609 B.C. The Bible tells us that in the 18th year of his reign (622 B.C.), he collected money from all the tribes, north and south, to make renovations to the Temple in Jerusalem. This was 100 years after the Assyrians had defeated the northern kingdom of Israel.

Chronicles reads:

When they came to Hilkiah the high priest, they delivered the money that was brought into the house of God, which the Levites who kept the doors had gathered from the hand of Manasseh and Ephraim, from all the remnant of Israel, from all Judah and Benjamin, and which they had brought back to Jerusalem (2 Chronicles 34:9).

In the same year, after Josiah had made the proper repairs to the Temple, he worshiped the Lord by celebrating a magnificent Passover. Tribes from both the north and the south participated:

> *There had been no Passover kept in Israel like that since the days of Samuel the prophet; and none of the kings of Israel had kept such a Passover as Josiah kept, with the priests and the Levites, all Judah and Israel who were present, and the inhabitants of Jerusalem. In the eighteenth year of the reign of Josiah this Passover was kept* (2 Chronicles 35:18-19).

Furthermore, when the southern exiles returned from their Babylonian captivity in 536 B.C., a remnant from the tribes of Ephraim and Manasseh returned with them:

> *Now in Jerusalem the children of Judah dwelt, and some of the children of Benjamin, and of the children of Ephraim and Manasseh...* (1 Chronicles 9:3).

In ancient as well as modern times, when a nation conquers another nation, the victor usually deports the leaders of the nation they conquered. The obvious reason is to remove the people who are most likely to lead a rebellion against them. This usually includes the intellectuals and thinkers and activists who pose a threat to the victor. The victor doesn't deport the common folk because they need them to do their work for them. The victor sends their own leaders to control the populace of the conquered nation. This means that when a nation is conquered by another, only a relatively small number of people are deported. This is what happened when both the northern and southern kingdoms were conquered by the Assyrians and the Babylonians.

While we can't know for sure, some scholars such as those published in *Biblical Archaeologist* noted below have estimated that the population of the northern kingdom of Israel was between 400,000 and 500,000 when the Assyrians conquered it. In 724 B.C., the Syrian King Shalmaneser V invaded the northern kingdom. The war lasted for three years. While Shalmaneser began the war, his successor, King Sargon II, finally defeated the northern kingdom in 721 B.C. This was in the ninth year of the reign of Hoshea, the last king of Israel. (See Second Kings 17.)

We are fortunate to have an historical record of the number deported. In September 1943, *Biblical Archaeologist* magazine published an article by H. G. May stating that archaeologists had discovered writings of King Sargon II. According to the writings, the king said that he only deported 27,290 people from the northern kingdom plus 50 chariots.[1] While the northern kingdom as a separate kingdom was lost, the great majority of the people remained in the land and kept their tribal identity. If the population in the northern kingdom was between 400,000 and 500,000, the number deported by King Sargon only amounted to from 5 to 7 percent of the total.

The real scattering of the Jewish people took place centuries later at the hands of the Romans. The first great scattering happened in A.D. 70 when the Roman Emperor Titus destroyed Jerusalem, burned down the Temple and dispersed the Jews throughout the Roman Empire. The second great scattering took place 65 years later (A.D. 135) when the Roman Emperor Hadrian defeated the Jews in the second Jewish war against the Romans. He banished the Jews from the land, renamed Israel Palestine, and made Jerusalem a pagan Roman city. While many Jews stayed in the land and moved out of harm's way, most were actually killed and others deported.

Modern DNA research validates that no matter where Jews live in the modern[2] world, they are kin and all come from the same geographic region of the world. That geographic region is Israel and the Middle East—and the Lord is returning them home to their ancient land.

REVIEW QUESTIONS

1. Write a summary of what you have learned in this lesson. Write the summary in clear, concise words as if you were going to present it to another person.

2. Write an explanation of how you can apply what you have learned in this lesson to your life.

3. Share what you have learned with your family, friends, and members of your study group.

ENDNOTES

1. H.G. May, "The Ten Lost Tribes," *Biblical Archaeologist* VI (1943), September 1943, 56-58.

2. Yaakov Klieman, "Jewish Genes," aish.com, (quoting M.F. Hammer, National Academy of Science, May 9, 2000), http://www.aish.com/ci/sam/48937817.html (accessed May 12, 2011).

Chapter 6

Israelites and Jews

REVELATION REVIEW

IN the previous chapter we discussed God's seal of protection placed on His people before the seventh seal was opened. As mentioned, the seventh seal opens the seven additional trumpet-shofar judgments, and the seventh trumpet-shofar opens the final seven bowl judgments. Because the further judgments are so severe, God seals His own for protection from His wrath against the unrighteous. Although most see this tribulation period as a time of doom and gloom, God's judgments are His response to the prayers of the saints who were martyred for their faith.

There is an example in the Book of Ezekiel of God marking His own before administering His judgments. When the Lord called His warring angels to judge the wicked, He had one of them put a mark on the forehead of the righteous. Those who had the mark of God would be protected from His wrath.

Ezekiel reads:

> *Now the glory of the God of Israel had gone up from the cherub, where it had been, to the threshold of the temple.*

And He called to the man clothed with linen, who had the writer's inkhorn at his side; and the LORD said to him, "Go through the midst of the city, through the midst of Jerusalem, and put a mark on the foreheads of the men who sigh and cry over all the abominations that are done within it." To the others He said in my hearing, "Go after him through the city and kill; do not let your eye spare, nor have any pity. Utterly slay old and young men, maidens and little children and women; but do not come near anyone on whom is the mark; and begin at My sanctuary." So they began with the elders who were before the temple (Ezekiel 9:3-6).

In the Book of Revelation, God will protect those He has marked or sealed from the last of the judgments against those who have the Mark of the Beast. Furthermore, there seems to be a third group that has neither the Mark of the Beast nor the sealing of God. Perhaps the people in this group have not yet dedicated themselves to the Lord, but don't want to take the Mark of the Beast. Only the Lord knows the details, but the overall picture is clear—God will reward the righteous and judge the unrighteous.

It is important that we distinguish between the judgment of God wrought on those who oppose Him and the persecution of believers by those who are unrighteous. While the Lord promises to protect His own from His coming wrath, He does not promise to protect believers from persecution. In fact, throughout history, persecution against believers has been the norm. Millions have been martyred for their witness to the One True God. This hatred of God and His people continues today as believers are being martyred throughout the world, particularly in Arab and African countries. For example, consider the Coptic Christians in Egypt as well as Christians in the Sudan. I personally believe we will see this in the West as Islamic fundamentalists gain more control of Europe and eventually North America.

We also learned the history of the ten lost tribes of Israel. According to the Bible, they were never lost. What was lost was Israel as an independent kingdom. While the northern kingdom of Israel ceased to exist, only a small remnant of the people (5 to 7 percent) were actually scattered. The real scattering came centuries later at the hands of the Romans. The Lord knows who they are and where they are and is bringing them home to Israel. The great majority of the people stayed in the land and kept their tribal identity, intermarried with the Assyrians (who had been placed in Israel to form the Samaritans), or migrated to Judah in the south.

ISRAELITES AND JEWS (REVELATION 4-8)

Because the kingdom was divided, people sometimes make a distinction between Israel (the northern kingdom) and Judah (the southern kingdom) and believe that only those of the tribe of Judah are truly Jews. Contributing to this thought is the fact that the name Judah in Hebrew is *Y'hudah* (also *Yehuwdah*)[1] from which we get the word *Jew*. The belief then is that the Israelites are not really Jews. While this may be a common understanding by some, the Bible does not make this distinction. We must look to the Bible and not man's opinions for truth. Let's read what the Bible says.

Because Ephraim was the dominant tribe in the northern kingdom, Israel was sometimes referred to as Ephraim. The words were often synonymous. Isaiah writes:

> *The LORD will bring the king of Assyria upon you and your people and your father's house—days that have not come since the day that Ephraim [Israel] departed from Judah (Isaiah 7:17; see also Ezek. 37:16-20).*

The Book of Ezra tells the story of the return of the captives from Babylon and the rebuilding of the Temple. The Book of Nehemiah continues the narrative from Ezra. In Ezra and Nehemiah, the word *Jews* is found 18 times while the word *Israel* is mentioned 62 times. In both Ezra and Nehemiah, the word *Jews* and the word *Israel* are referring to the same company of people. The words are used interchangeably. Neither Ezra nor Nehemiah makes a distinction between Israel (Ephraim) and Judah (Jews). They are one people. You can look this up for yourself to see how the words are used.

In the New Testament, the word *Israel* is used 75 times and the word *Jews* 174 times. These words are generally used interchangeably and refer to the descendants of Jacob—the children of Israel. There is not a clear distinction and separation of Israel (Ephraim) and Judah (Jews) as some believe.

In the New Testament, the word *Jew(s)* is sometimes used in the narrowest sense and refers to the Jewish establishment in Jerusalem. It does not refer to the Jewish people in general. This is very important to understand. When the New Testament says that *the Jews* killed Jesus the writers are talking about the establishment, not the people. For example, John writes:

> *After these things Jesus walked in Galilee; for He did not want to walk in Judea, because the Jews sought to kill Him* (John 7:1).

It is important to understand that John did not mean all the Jews but the Sadducees (the High Priest and his followers) who were in charge of the Temple.

The New Testament confirms that the 12 tribes were not lost and were considered to be one people. James writes his letter to the 12 tribes scattered abroad (see James 1:1). This was when the believers were being persecuted and many scattered from Jerusalem. By then, Jewish believers were living in Israel while others were living among the Gentiles in the surrounding countries. James does not distinguish between Israelites and Jews.

When Paul appeared before King Agrippa he spoke of the 12 tribes as one company of people, saying, *"To this promise our twelve tribes, earnestly serving God night and day, hope to attain..."* (Acts 26:7).

Furthermore, Paul referred to himself as both a Jew and an Israelite. When addressing a mob in Jerusalem Paul said:

> *I am indeed a Jew, born in Tarsus of Cilicia, but brought up in this city at the feet of Gamaliel, taught according to the strictness of our fathers' law, and was zealous toward God as you all are today* (Acts 22:3).

In Romans he wrote:

> *I say then, has God cast away His people? Certainly not! For I also am an Israelite, of the seed of Abraham, of the tribe of Benjamin* (Romans 11:1).

In Romans 9:4 Paul uses the word *Israelites* and clearly means all of the children of Israel not just those from the tribe of Judah. He never makes a distinction between Israelites and Jews. To him, the words are synonymous.

To return to the Book of Revelation, all 12 tribes are listed. None are lost. In Revelation 21:12 we learn that the gates of the New Heavenly Jerusalem have the names of the 12 tribes on them. Furthermore, Ezekiel 48 gives the allotment of the land to the children of Israel during the Messianic Kingdom, saying, *"Thus you shall divide the land among yourselves according to the tribes of Israel"* (Ezek. 47:21). Ezekiel then lists all 12 tribes including Dan and Ephraim (with Manasseh and Ephraim being counted as one tribe). (See Ezekiel 48.)

Ezekiel also mentions the strangers who dwell with the children of Israel and says that they will receive an inheritance among the tribes:

"It shall be that you will divide it [the land] *by lot as an inheritance for yourselves, and for the strangers who dwell among you and who bear children among you. They shall be to you as native-born among the children of Israel; they shall have an inheritance with you among the tribes of Israel. And it shall be that in whatever tribe the stranger dwells, there you shall give him his inheritance,"* says the Lord GOD (Ezekiel 47:22-23).

The strangers are the non-Jewish believers (Christians) who are part of the Commonwealth of Israel as previously mentioned and written in Ephesians 2:11-22. When Ezekiel was writing, the non-Jews who joined themselves to the Jews were called strangers. However, Paul says that, through Messiah, we are no longer strangers or foreigners; instead we are fellow citizens (see Eph. 2:19). Christians have joined themselves with the children of Israel by which they have become part of the Israel of God. Hallelujah! They are not the Israel of God but they have joined themselves as one with Israel (see Gal. 6:16.)

EPHRAIM—A MULTITUDE OF NATIONS

Because historians and scholars have wrongly assumed that the ten tribes to the north were scattered en masse and lost, there have been many attempts to try to identify these supposed lost tribes. All of these efforts are based on a misunderstanding of a few Scriptures in the Book of Genesis. As just discussed, some were scattered. The Lord has preserved their identity and is bringing them home to Israel. But as we have just read in the Bible, there was never such a large scattering of the ten tribes that they lost their identity and became Gentiles.

One of the most popular theories that developed in the 19th century is that the "ten lost tribes" are the ancestors of the British. This theory is called the British-Israelite theory which teaches that the supposed lost tribes migrated to Britain and became the Anglo-Saxons. Since Britain ruled the world at that time, this theory taught that Britain and its commonwealth of nations were the ten lost tribes of Israel that inherited the promises God made to Abraham. This is the ultimate in replacement theology. Of course Britain is no longer an empire; neither does it have a political commonwealth of nations.

The British-Israelite theory was embraced and taught in the United States by the World Wide Church of God founded by Herbert Armstrong. Because the United States was founded by immigrants from Britain, this view considers European Americans and certain Christians to be Ephraimites. When Herbert Armstrong died, his followers scattered and took this teaching with them to Christian groups they joined. Joseph Smith also embraced this idea, which became an early teaching of the Mormons.

With all due respect, there is absolutely no biblical or historical basis to support these teachings. It takes a big imagination, a willingness to overlook the biblical text and a lack of knowledge of history to believe that Joseph's two sons, Ephraim and Manasseh, became Britain and America. While there are millions of Hispanics with Jewish roots from the Inquisition who are Jewish, and some American and European Gentiles have Jewish ancestry, for the most part, Jews are Jews and Gentiles are Gentiles.

I want to explain a few Scriptures in Genesis that relate to this subject and are often misinterpreted. As we will see, the English words are very misleading. But when we take the time to look up the Hebrew words, these confusing Scriptures are simple and easy to understand. They are so simple that we sometimes miss their meaning and complicate them by trying to make them fit into our unscriptural theories.

Let's began with the word for "nation(s)." The Hebrew word is *goy(im)*.[2] This word is found many times in the Bible. This is a generic word that simply refers to any ethnic group of people, although the concordance takes the modern view and places the emphasis on Gentiles.

Because the Jewish people have suffered throughout the centuries at the hands of the nations, the Jews began to apply the word *goy* exclusively to the Gentiles—the nations as opposed to the Jews. However, in the early history of the Jewish people, this was not the case. Now here is a shock. In the Bible, the word *goy(im)* is not only used for Gentiles; it is also used to refer to the Jews. Wow! That was a revelation for me. How about you? There are far too many references to *nations(s)* and *goy(im)* to discuss every one. That is not necessary. We want to look up a few that are relevant to this discussion.

One of the most significant Scripture passages that all Bible readers are familiar with tells the story of when God called Abraham to leave his home and go to a land that God would give him. Abraham was 75 years of age at the time. Genesis reads:

> Now the LORD had said to Abram: "Get out of your country, from your family and from your father's house, to a land that I will show you. I will make you a great nation [goy]; I will bless you and make your name great; and you shall be a blessing. I will bless those who bless you, and I will curse him who curses you; and in you all the families of the earth shall be blessed" (Genesis 12:1-3).

Notice that the word used to refer to Abraham's natural descendants is *goy*. It simply means that God will give Abraham many descendants who will became an ethnic people—the Jews, the people God called to be a light to the nations. The Lord further encourages Abraham with the promise of many descendants in Genesis 13:14-16. Whenever God tells Abraham and his children that they will have many descendants, He simply means they will be a fruitful people *(goy).*

When Abraham was 99 years of age, God appeared to him again to confirm His covenant. Genesis reads:

When Abram was ninety-nine years old, the Lord appeared to Abram and said to him, "I am Almighty God; walk before Me and be blameless. And I will make My covenant between Me and you, and will multiply you exceedingly."

Then Abram fell on his face, and God talked with him, saying: "As for Me, behold, My covenant is with you, and you shall be a father of many nations [goyim]. *No longer shall your name be called Abram, but your name shall be Abraham; for I have made you a father of many nations* [goyim]. *I will make you exceedingly fruitful; and I will make nations* [goyim, fruitful ethnic tribes] *of you, and kings shall come from you. And I will establish My covenant between Me and you and your descendants after you in their generations, for an everlasting covenant, to be God to you and your descendants after you"* (Genesis 17:1-7).

Notice that when the Lord confirmed His covenant with Abraham, He changed his name from Abram to Abraham. Abram means father or patriarch but Abraham means father of a multitude. This simply means that God would bless Abraham to be the father of many ethnic peoples or descendants *(goyim)*.

The Lord then revealed to Abraham that he and Sarah would have a child even though Sarah was past the age of childbearing:

Then God said to Abraham, "As for Sarai you wife, you shall not call her name Sarai, but Sarah shall be her name. And I will bless her and also give you a son by her; then I will bless her, and she shall be a mother of nations [goyim, as in fruitful ethnic tribes]; *kings of peoples shall be from her"* (Genesis 17:15-16).

The Lord changed Sarah's name to make her part of the covenant with her husband. He promised Sarah, that although she was barren, she would have a son (Isaac) and be the mother of many nations (*goyim*, fruitful ethnic tribes). Furthermore, kings who would rule over these tribes would also come from her womb. God was referring to the 12 tribes of Israel and the many descendants who would come from them. He clearly was not talking about Gentiles.

In Genesis 18, the Lord again appeared to Abraham and told him of His plan to destroy Sodom. In this Scripture, we see the word *goy(im)* used to refer both to Abraham's descendants and the Gentile nations. The Scripture reads:

> *And the Lord said, "Shall I hide from Abraham what I am doing, since Abraham shall surely become a great and mighty nation* [goy, referring to the Jews], *and all the nations* [goyim, referring to the Gentiles] *of the earth shall be blessed in him?"* (Genesis 18:17-18).

Later, God instructed Abraham to offer his son Isaac as a sacrifice. When Abraham obeyed, the Lord reconfirmed His promise to give Abraham many descendants. He also said that Abraham's seed (the Messiah) would be a blessing to the whole world. In this instance, the word translated "nations" refers to the Gentiles. Genesis reads:

> *in blessing I will bless you, and in multiplying I will multiply your descendants as the stars of the heaven and as the sand which is on the seashore; and your descendants shall possess the gate of their enemies. In your seed* [singular, referring to the Messiah] *all the* nations [goyim, referring to the Gentiles] *of the earth shall be blessed, because you have obeyed My voice* (Genesis 22:17-18).

When it was known that Rebekah would become the bride of Isaac, her family sent her off with this blessing of fruitfulness:

And they blessed Rebekah and said to her: "Our sister, may you become the mother of thousands of ten thousands; and may your descendants possess the gates of those who hate them" (Genesis 24:60).

The Lord made the same promise of fruitfulness to Isaac:

Dwell in this land, and I will be with you and bless you; for to you and your descendants I give all these lands, and I will perform the oath which I swore to Abraham your father. And I will make your descendants multiply as the stars of heaven; I will give to your descendants all these lands; and in your seed all the nations [goyim, referring to the Gentiles] *of the earth shall be blessed* (Genesis 26:3-4).

The Lord continued the promise of the land and fruitfulness to Jacob. His father, Isaac, spoke the following blessings:

May God Almighty bless you, and make you fruitful and multiply you, that you may be an assembly of peoples; and give you the blessing of Abraham, to you and your descendants with you, that you may inherit the land in which you are a stranger, which God gave to Abraham.

Also your descendants shall be as the dust of the earth; you shall spread abroad to the west and the east, to the north and the south; and in you and in your seed all the families of the earth shall be blessed (Genesis 28:3-4;14-15).

Later, God changed Jacob's name to Israel and repeated the promise of fruitfulness:

And God said to him, "Your name is Jacob; your name shall not be called Jacob anymore, but Israel shall be your

*name." So He called his name Israel. Also God said to him,
"I am God Almighty. Be fruitful and multiply; a nation
[goy] and a company of nations [goyim, fruitful ethnic
tribes] shall proceed from you, and kings shall come from
your body. The land which I gave Abraham and Isaac I
give to you; and to your descendants after you I give this
land"* (Genesis 35:10-12).

I have taken this extra time to quote all these Scriptures to clearly show that the same word, *goy(im)*, is used for both the natural ethnic descendants of Abraham, Isaac, and Jacob (who became the 12 tribes of Israel), and the Gentile nations. We now move forward to explain the one Scripture that is often misinterpreted due primarily to the unfortunate English translation.

Bible students know that Joseph's brothers sold him into slavery and he ended up in Egypt. After Joseph was vindicated, Pharaoh made him his chief assistant or prime minister. While in Egypt, Joseph married and had two sons:

*Joseph called the name of the first-born Manasseh: "For
God has made me forget all my toil and all my father's
house." And the name of the second he called Ephraim:
"For God has caused me to be fruitful in the land of my
affliction"* (Genesis 41:51-52).

In Bible times, people named their children with a significance that pertained to the issues in their lives. Joseph named his firstborn Manasseh. *Manasseh* means "causing to forget."[3] The idea is that the birth of Manasseh helped Joseph to forget all the troubles he had in his earlier life. He named his second-born Ephraim. *Ephraim* means "fruitfulness"[4] or "double fruit"[5] because he is the second son born to Joseph. These names also are prophetic in that both Manasseh's and Ephraim's descendants would forget their covenant with God and would also have many descendants. They would be fruitful.

When Jacob was about to die, Joseph went to him and brought his two sons so Jacob could bless them. Joseph was Jacob's favorite son. In view of this, Jacob adopted Joseph's sons as his own because he wanted to give Joseph the double-portion blessing of having two sons inherit the land rather than just Joseph. Although they would become two tribes, they were considered as one son of Joseph.

In Genesis 48, Jacob makes God's promise and his own wishes known to Joseph:

> ...Jacob said to Joseph: "God Almighty appeared to me at
> Luz in the land of Canaan and blessed me, and said to
> me, 'Behold, I will make you fruitful and multiply you,
> and I will make you a multitude of people, and give this
> land to your descendants after you as an everlasting pos-
> session. And now your two sons, Ephraim and Manasseh,
> who were born to you in the land of Egypt before I came to
> you in Egypt, are mine; as Reuben and Simeon, they shall
> be mine'" (Genesis 48:3-5).

It was customary for the father to put his right hand of blessing on the head of the firstborn (the oldest). So when Joseph presented his sons to his father, Joseph put Manasseh on the left side in front of Jacob's right hand. He put Ephraim on the right side in front of Jacob's left hand. But when Jacob, now called Israel, went to bless them, he crossed his hands and put his right hand of the firstborn blessing on Ephraim and his left hand on Manasseh (see Gen. 48:13-14).

Jacob then pronounced this blessing over Joseph:

> And he blessed Joseph, and said: "God, before whom my
> fathers Abraham and Isaac walked, the God who has fed
> me all my life long to this day, the Angel who has redeemed
> me from all evil, bless the lads; let my name be named
> upon them, and the name of my fathers Abraham and

Isaac; and let them grow into a multitude in the midst of the earth" (Genesis 48:15-16).

Joseph was alarmed and thought his father was confused. He even started to switch Jacob's hands, but Jacob would not allow it:

But his father refused and said, "I know my son, I know. He [Manasseh] *also shall become a people, and he also shall be great; but truly his younger brother* [Ephraim] *shall be greater than he, and his descendants shall become a multitude of nations* [goyim, referring to many descendants]*." So he blessed them that day, saying, "By you Israel will bless, saying, 'May God make you as Ephraim and as Manasseh!'" And thus he set Ephraim before Manasseh* (Genesis 48:19-20).

The confusing wording is the phrase Jacob spoke over Ephraim: *"... his descendants shall become a multitude of nations."* Those who believe that the ten tribes were scattered and lost believe this prophecy to mean that Ephraim's descendants (also called Israel) became Gentiles living among the nations (*goyim*).

However, as I have substantiated in the previous chapter, the Scriptures clearly say and history confirms that only a small remnant of the ten tribes was actually deported. The majority either stayed in the north, intermarried with the people sent there by the Assyrians, or moved to the south. We have also clearly seen that the word *goy(im)* is a general word that simply means an ethnic group—any ethnic group. In the Bible, it is used to refer to the Jews and the Gentiles.

What this phrase simply means is that Ephraim will be fruitful and have a lot of descendants. It is the same promise God made to Abraham, Isaac, Jacob, Sarah, and Rebekah. The Lord used almost the same words in all these promises. He said that He would make them a great nation (*goy*); He said that many nations (*goyim*, or fruitful ethnic tribes) would come from them; He said they would have many descendants, they would be a multitude of people, they would be a multitude in the midst of the earth, they would be exceedingly fruitful, etc.

These prophecies were fulfilled in the natural descendants of Abraham, Isaac, and Jacob who became the 12 tribes of the children of Israel. Ephraim and Manasseh combined became the largest of the tribes. In the Book of Numbers, the first census established the numbers of those in each tribe who were 20 years and older and able to go to war. Together, Ephraim and Manasseh, representing the single tribe of Joseph numbered 72,700 (see Num. 1:33, 35). A second census was taken later and the combined number of Ephraim and Manasseh was 85,200 (see Num. 26:34, 37). When the tribes finally received their inheritance in the land, the descendants of Ephraim were the most influential—so much so that the northern kingdom of Israel was also called Ephraim.

Jewish people, as well as Christians who are discovering their roots, know that fruitfulness is the meaning of Jacob's prophecy over Ephraim. Every Sabbath they lay their hands on their sons' heads and pray the same blessing that Jacob said over Ephraim and Manasseh, "May God make you as Ephraim and as Manasseh." In other words, may you be fruitful and multiply.

As just noted, the 12 gates of the New Jerusalem bear the names of the 12 tribes of Israel (see Rev. 21:12). The foundation of the city bears the names of the 12 apostles (see Rev. 21:14). While the 12 apostles were Jews, they brought the message of salvation to the Gentiles. These represent Jewish believers (descendants of Shem) and non-Jewish believers (descendants of Japheth and Ham) whom God has made one new man in Messiah. May His name be praised forever. Amen!

Review Questions

1. Write a summary of what you have learned in this lesson. Write the summary in clear, concise words as if you were going to present it to another person.

2. Write an explanation of how you can apply what you have learned in this lesson to your life.

3. Share what you have learned with your family, friends, and members of your study group.

Endnotes

1. Biblesoft's New Exhaustive Strong's Numbers and Concordance with Expanded Greek-Hebrew Dictionary. CD-ROM. Biblesoft, Inc. and International Bible Translators, Inc. (1994, 2003, 2006) s.v. "Yehuwdah," (O.T. 3063).

2. See, Ibid., (O.T. 1471) and *Blue Letter Bible,* Dictionary and Word Search for *"gowy"* (Strong's 1471), 1996-2011, <http://www.blueletterbible.org/lang/lexicon/lexicon.cfm? Strongs=H1471&t=KJV > (accessed May 5, 2011).

3. Biblesoft's New Exhaustive Strong's, s.v. "Manasseh," (O.T. 4519).

4. Ephraim is a form of *Ephraath.* Biblesoft's New Exhaustive Strong's, s.v. "Ephraath," (O.T. 672).

5. Biblesoft's New Exhaustive Strong's, s.v. "Ephrayim," (O.T. 669).

Chapter 7

The Multitude of the Redeemed

REVELATION REVIEW

IN the Hebrew Bible, the Lord called Abraham and his descendants through Isaac and Jacob to be a light to the nations. Unfortunately, history has shown us that the nations have not wanted God's light. In their effort to put out the light, the nations, often led by Christendom, have persecuted the Jews for centuries.

I have often heard my Jewish friends ask, "Why does the world hate us so much?" The world hates the Jews because the Jews remind them of God. World leaders have tried for centuries to destroy the Jews. They have failed because God gave His promise that He would preserve a remnant of Jewish people until the end of days.

Jeremiah reads:

Thus says the LORD, who gives the sun for a light by day, and the ordinances of the moon and the stars for a light by night, who disturbs the sea, and its waves roar (the LORD of hosts is His name): "If those ordinances depart from before Me, says the LORD, then the seed of Israel shall also cease from being a nation before Me forever." Thus says the LORD: "If heaven above can be measured, and the foundations of the earth searched out beneath, I will also cast off all the seed of Israel for all that they have done, says the LORD" (Jeremiah 31:35-37).

While neither Jews nor Christians have always let their light shine, the end times will be our greatest time to shine. Even though the time of tribulation is a time of great suffering, it will also be the time of the greatest spiritual awakening and revival the world has ever known.

The tribulation period is not a time of doom and gloom, but of the greatest outpouring of the glory of God the world has ever known. As John reveals, the number of people coming to the Lord during this time is so great, they are too many to count. Let's now read John's words describing these tribulation saints.

The Multitude of the Redeemed
(Revelation 7:9-17)

A Great Multitude (verses 9-12)

John describes a great multitude of believers. Because he says they come from *"all nations, tribes, peoples, and tongues,"* we know that he is not just talking about Jewish people coming to the Lord. He is also talking about millions upon millions of Gentiles. John says that he sees a great multitude which *"no one could number."* Wow, talk about exciting times.

In his apocalyptic vision, John sees these believers standing before the throne of God and the Lamb. As I was reading John's words, I wondered what it must be like to stand before the throne of God and the Lamb. Then I remembered John's vision of the throne of God and the

Lamb which he described in chapters 4 and 5. There John saw the blazing glory and dazzling beauty of God and the Son of Man with all of Heaven worshiping the Lord and giving praise to the Lamb.

In our current passage, John looks ahead to the end of this time of tribulation and sees this great multitude with the hosts of Heaven at the throne of God. Wow again! This leaves me breathless. As I see this scene with my own spiritual eyes, the magnificent majesty and spectacular splendor of it all are almost more than my earthly body can contain. Just contemplating standing before the throne of God makes any earthly suffering pale in the light of God's glorious presence with all the hosts of Heaven worshiping Him in the beauty of His holiness.

These overcoming saints of God are clothed with white robes and have palm branches in their hands. Remember that the Lord promised the faithful in the congregation at Sardis that He would clothe them in white robes and that they would walk with Him in white (see Rev. 3:4-5). He counseled the congregation at Laodicea to clothe themselves in white garments (see Rev. 3:18). In Revelation 4:4 we were told that the elders around the throne of God were clothed in white robes.

In the fifth seal, the martyrs were given white robes (see Rev. 6:11). When they cried out for justice, the Lord told them they had to wait until their fellow servants and brethren joined them (see Rev. 6:10-11). It may be that this great multitude are the fellow servants and brethren the Lord meant. Later, in Revelation 19:14, John sees the armies of Heaven *"clothed in fine linen, white and clean."*

Colors have symbolic meaning in the Bible. Blue represents the color of Heaven; scarlet the color of sacrifice; green the color of life; purple the color of royalty; white the color of purity. All of these overcomers are said to be clothed in white because the people of John's time understood what this meant. They had been clothed with the white garment of salvation and robe of righteousness, and they were pure in their hearts.

In Psalm 24, King David asked a question and then gave his own answer. He said:

> *Who may ascend into the hill of the LORD? Or who may stand in His holy place? He who has clean hands and a pure heart, Who has not lifted up his soul to an idol, Nor sworn deceitfully. He shall receive blessing from the LORD, And righteousness from the God of his salvation* (Psalm 24:3-5).

King David was talking about standing in the presence of God, be it on the earth or in Heaven. He said those who have clean hands and a pure heart can be in the presence of God; so what does it mean to have clean hands and a pure heart?

When we were children, our mothers taught us to wash our hands before eating a meal. The purpose of course was to literally and physically have clean hands. This is a matter of good hygiene; our mothers did not want us to handle our food with hands that were dirty or contaminated by germs. This was certainly a necessity in the time of King David when people ate with their hands and fingers. People in India and other places in the world still eat this way today.

But there is more to our hands than just having them clean physically. Spiritually speaking, our hands represent our service to our God. To have clean hands means that we have allowed the Holy Spirit to sanctify our service to the Lord. To sanctify means to set apart as holy to the Lord. In the Bible, to have clean hands means that we use our bodies in service to God in holiness so that we are not contaminated with the spiritual germs of worldliness.

There is a powerful Jewish tradition at their Sabbath meal that makes this connection of clean hands to the presence of God. To the Jewish people, the Sabbath meal is much more than just eating. The meal is considered a table of fellowship and reconciliation with God and family. It is a celebration of worship.

In his wonderful book, *God in Search of Man*, Abraham Joshua Heschel, of blessed memory, wrote, "Every home can be a temple, every table an altar, and all of life a song to God."[1]

The table (meal time) is considered an altar—a place of worship and fellowship. It is interesting that the Hebrew word for table means reconciliation. In view of this spiritual connection of our hands to holy service to God, it is customary to have a ritual hand washing before eating the Sabbath meal. The blessing prayer for the hand washing is:

Baruch ata Adonai, Eloheynu Melech Haolam, asher kidshanu bemitzvotav, vetzivanu al netilat yadayim.[2]

The English translation is:

Blessed are You O Lord, our God, King of the universe, who has sanctified us with His commandments, and has commanded (or inspired) us regarding washing hands."[3]

Once again, from *God in Search of Man*, Heschel makes the clear connection between the outward ritual and the spiritual reality, "The goal is not that a ceremony be performed; the goal is that man be transformed; to worship the Holy in order to be holy. The purpose of the *mitsvot* [good deeds] is to sanctify man."[4]

The apostle Paul was a Jew. He would have memorized the whole of the Hebrew Bible including King David's statement regarding clean hands in Psalm 24. Paul knew what it meant spiritually to have clean hands. It was his Jewish background that prompted him to say:

I beseech you therefore, brethren, by the mercies of God, that you present your bodies a living sacrifice, holy, acceptable to God, which is your reasonable service. And do not be conformed to this world, but be transformed by the renewing of your mind, that you may prove what is that good and acceptable and perfect will of God (Romans 12:1-2).

This great multitude of believers can stand before the throne of God and before the Lamb because they have clean hands. They have presented their bodies as holy, living sacrifices to God. The Lord has made this promise to all who serve Him in the beauty of holiness.

In Psalm 24 King David also mentioned the necessity of serving God with a pure heart. Jesus must have been alluding to this Scripture when He said, *"Blessed are the pure in heart, for they shall see God"* (Matt. 5:8).

Oh, to be pure in heart. What does this mean? The Bible gives us several word pictures of what it means to be pure in heart. One relates to mining for gold. When looking for gold, the prospector pans or shovels material from the water or the earth. This material may contain gold but it will also contain other material such as rocks, sediment, other metals, and an assortment of foreign substances. In other words, it is not all pure gold.

It is necessary for the prospector to separate the gold from the foreign matter. The way he does this is to put the material in a crucible, which is a pot that he places over a very hot fire. It is a melting pot. Most of the material falls to the bottom of the pot, making the melting liquid murky.

The prospector then looks into the pot to see if he can see his face reflected in the melting liquid. If he cannot see his face clearly, he knows that there is more foreign material in the bottom of the pot. He turns up the fire under the pot which causes the unwanted material to rise to the top. The prospector then removes this material from the crucible. Then he again looks into the melting liquid to see his face. As long as he cannot see his face clearly, he knows that there is more foreign matter at the bottom of the crucible that must be removed.

The prospector continues to turn up the fire to bring up the foreign matter and remove it from the crucible. This is the origin of the term "skimming off the top." He repeats this action until he can see his face clearly in the melted liquid. At that point, he knows the only thing left in the crucible is pure gold.

Job was a man who suffered greatly. He had experienced the crucible of life. He understood that the testing he endured was to purify his heart. He wrote:

> *Look, I go forward, but He is not there, and backward, but I cannot perceive Him; when He works on the left hand, I cannot behold Him; when He turns to the right hand, I cannot see Him. But He knows the way that I take; when He has tested me, I shall come forth as gold* (Job 23:8-10).

Job was looking for God. He wanted to be in His presence but He could not perceive God. Yet, Job understood the process. He knew that when God had refined him, he would have a pure heart and could behold God in the beauty of His holiness. This promise of being in God's presence enabled him to persevere in his time of testing.

Like Job, the great multitude in Revelation 7 has been through the crucible of tribulation. Their hearts have been tested. Their motives are pure. Their love and service to God and their testimony have been real, without pretense, without an agenda, without a selfish motive, without self-glory, and without wanting anything in return. They can stand before the presence of God and see Him face to face (see Rev. 22:4). They can do this because when God sees them, He sees Himself. They are like Him because they have clean hands and pure hearts.

The prophet Malachi spoke of God being a refiner and wrote that only God's people who are pure will be able to stand in the day of His coming:

But who can endure the day of His coming? And who can stand when He appears? For He is like a refiner's fire and like launderers' soap. He will sit as a refiner and a purifier of silver; He will purify the sons of Levi, and purge them as gold and silver, that they may offer to the LORD an offering in righteousness (Malachi 3:2-3).

The apostle Paul wrote:

For we must all appear before the judgment seat of Christ [Messiah], *that each one may receive the things done in the body, according to what he has done, whether good* [acceptable to God] *or bad* [unacceptable to God] (2 Corinthians 5:10).

Paul also explained that…

each one's work will become clear; for the Day will declare it, because it will be revealed by fire; and the fire will test each one's work, of what sort it is (1 Corinthians 3:13).

Believers do many good works but not always for the right reasons. Sometimes the motives of our hearts are not pure. As we see The Day approaching, we certainly want to make sure that our motives are pure and will stand the test of fire. So let us examine our hearts in this regard. If we are not experiencing the presence of God, perhaps we need to ask the Holy Spirit to skim any impurities (wrong motives) from our hearts.

James gave a blunt word that we should all receive with meekness and humility:

Draw near to God and He will draw near to you. Cleanse your hands, you sinners; and purify your hearts, you double-minded. Lament and mourn and weep! Let your laughter be turned to mourning and your joy to gloom.

Humble yourselves in the sight of the Lord, and He will lift you up (James 4:8-10).

May the Lord help us to have clean hands and pure hearts. May it be that when we stand in His presence with the great multitude of saints, our works of love will stand the test of fire. May we live with this vision burning in our hearts, knowing that one day we will be like Him, for we will see Him face to face.

As we have just noted, Jesus said in Matthew 5:8 that the pure in heart will see God. While Jesus would have spoken Hebrew, His words were soon translated into Greek for a Greek-speaking world. There are a number of different Greek words in the New Testament which are translated into English as "see." Some of the words mean to see from a distance, or to see with a blur or to see with a casual notice. The Greek word used to translate what Jesus said means to see clearly, with eyes wide open, staring intently with awe and wonder,[5] or as we sometimes say, "up close and personal."

We can relate to the example of looking at a distant object through a telescope. When we first look through the telescope, the object appears to be very far away and out of focus. We don't know what we are seeing because it is not clear. We extend the telescope so we can see the object more clearly. This extension usually brings the object into sharper focus, but it is still not really clear. So we extend the telescope further until the object is magnified enough to be in clear focus. Even though the object is far away, the extension of the telescope makes it seem close at hand.

This is what Jesus meant when He said that the pure in heart will see God. He didn't mean we would vaguely see God from a distance. He meant that the telescope of our eyes will be fully extended. He meant that we will see God clearly with our eyes wide open. He meant that we will be staring intently at God's face with awe and wonder. He meant that we will be "up close and personal" with our Father in Heaven.

Wow! Now that ought to be enough to make us want to have clean hands and pure hearts.

John also informs us that the great multitude has palm branches in their hands. What would this mean to John's readers? In his time, palm branches were often used as a symbol of victory. In Greek and Roman athletic events, winners were given palm branches by the judges. It was a great honor to have a palm branch in your hands. That palm branch not only represented your victory, but all the hard work, discipline, and commitment you endured to overcome your competitors.

The Jews adopted this practice. We recall the story of Jesus entering Jerusalem during Passover. John tells us that a great multitude came out to greet Jesus. They had palm branches to wave toward Him as they fully expected Him to start the revolution that would overthrow the Romans.

This same John reports:

> The next day a great multitude that had come to the feast, when they heard that Jesus was coming to Jerusalem, took branches of palm trees and went out to meet Him, and cried out, "Hosanna! Blessed is He who comes in the name of the LORD! The King of Israel!" (John 12:12-13).

The crowd was alluding to the following psalm:

> Save now, I pray, O LORD; O LORD, I pray, send now prosperity. Blessed is he who comes in the name of the LORD!...God is the LORD, and He has given us light; bind the sacrifice with cords to the horns of the altar. You are my God, and I will praise You... Oh give thanks to the LORD, for He is good! For His mercy endures forever (Psalm 118:25-29).

The phrase, "Save now" is the English equivalent for the Hebrew translated in the Matthew verse as "Hosanna." Many in the crowds had witnessed Jesus raising Lazarus from the dead. They were now calling on Him to save them physically and spiritually from their human suffering as well as from the Romans.

As we know, the people were disappointed because Jesus did not come to overthrow the Romans. We can understand their disappointment. Jesus came as the Lamb of God to die for our sins. This crowd was so desperate and so full of expectation that they forget the rest of the psalm which says, *"bind the sacrifice with cords to the horns of the altar"* (Ps. 118:27). This pointed to the Messiah being crucified. As Father Abraham bound his only uniquely born son Isaac to the horns of the altar (see Gen. 22:9), so our Father God bound His only uniquely born Son to the altar of the crucifixion tree.

Just as Jesus overcame satan, sin, and death, these tribulation believers also overcame their persecutors. Let us understand clearly that these believers were not victims, but victors—winners in their righteous struggle to live for God during difficult times. The Judge of the living and the dead gives them palm branches as a symbol of their triumph over evil.

These overcomers most certainly wave their palm branches before the exalted Son of Man just as the enthusiastic crowd did when they greeted Jesus in Jerusalem 2,000 years ago. They too sang the song of salvation to God and to the Lamb. All of Heaven hears their voices crying out to the Lord, "Save now! Hosanna! Salvation belongs to God and to the Lamb." The difference is that this multitude now knows the Lamb as the Lion of the Tribe of Judah.

In this heavenly scene, Jesus is not the baby in the manger; He is the King who is coming to judge the earth and make war against those who oppose the purposes of God (see Rev. 19:11). Despite the foolish decrees of the one world globalists who want to displace God and kill His people, God is going to rule over the nations. They will acknowledge Him as the only Sovereign King.

As a psalm of David explains:

All the ends of the world shall remember and turn to the LORD, and all the families of the nations shall worship before You. For the Kingdom is the LORD's, and He rules over the nations (Psalm 22:27-28).

These believers have proven themselves to be faithful and will rule with the Lord over those who have persecuted them. As we learned earlier, when Jesus took the scroll from the right hand of His Father, those in His presence from all the nations...

...sang a new song, saying: "You are worthy to take the scroll, and to open its seals; for You were slain, and have redeemed us to God by Your blood out of every tribe and tongue and people and nation, and have made us kings and priests to our God; and we shall reign on the earth" (Revelation 5:9-10).

When this company of the redeemed sings their song of salvation, the angels around the throne, the elders, and the four special living beings fall on their faces before the throne of God and worship Him as they did earlier. John is most privileged to see and hear this incredible scene. And he records it for us so we can join with them, saying:

...Amen! Blessing and glory and wisdom, thanksgiving and honor and power and might, be to our God forever and ever. Amen (Revelation 7:12).

This is almost the same worship they gave to the Lord in Revelation 5:12:

Worthy is the Lamb who was slain to receive power and riches and wisdom, and strength and honor and glory and blessing!

(Notice that the word *thanksgiving* from the former verse is replaced in the latter with the word *riches*.)

What an incredible scene. This is what God's people have to look forward to. While the future is doom and gloom for those who oppose God, believers have a glorious future living forever in His presence!

As Jude wrote in His praise to God:

> *Now to Him who is able to keep you from stumbling* [fall-ing], *and to present you faultless before the presence of His glory with exceeding joy, to God our Savior, who alone is wise, be glory and majesty, dominion and power, both now and forever. Amen* (Jude 24-25).

Identifying the Great Multitude (verses 13-17)

In the midst of this incredible worship and praise, one of the elders asks John if he knows who all these people are and where they came from. Perhaps this question was to encourage those who would read John's vision because they were enduring tremendous persecution. The elder wanted them to have a sure hope that the overcomers have a glorious future. God understood their sufferings. It would only last for awhile, but their heavenly blessings would be forever.

So the elder and John are like a team in which one person asks the question so the other person can give the answer for the audience. Here John plays the role of the one who gives the cue for the elder to answer. The elder identifies the people as those overcomers who came out of the Great Tribulation.

It is important to note that, in spite of the best and most honorable efforts of leaders who try to bring world peace through the New World Order, man's efforts will only bring more suffering. World leaders do not recognize the sinful nature of human beings who do not want God ruling over them. Since Bible-believing Jews and Christians oppose them, the New World Order leaders will persecute God's people.

This time of unparalleled hate against God's people will begin gradually but, once in place, their fanatical desire to control the lives of everyone results in a "police state" much like Nazi Germany. The result is a time of chaos and suffering like the world has never known.

Students of the Bible refer to this period of time as "the tribulation." Most Bible scholars believe this is the last seven years of our present world order and ends at the coming of Jesus. Since the persecution against believers intensifies toward the end of these seven years, the last half of this period is referred to as *The Great Tribulation.*

The Hebrew prophet Daniel had an apocalyptic vision of this time. An angel revealed this to Daniel and explained:

> *At that time Michael* [the guardian angel of Israel] *shall stand up, the great prince who stands watch over the sons of your people; and there shall be a time of trouble, such as never was since there was a nation, even to that time. And at that time your people shall be delivered, every one who is found written in the book. And many of those who sleep in the dust of the earth shall awake* [be resurrected], *some to everlasting life, some to shame and everlasting contempt. Those who are wise shall shine like the brightness of the firmament, and those who turn many to righteousness like the stars forever and ever. But you, Daniel, shut up the words, and seal the book until the time of the end; many shall run to and fro, and knowledge shall increase* (Daniel 12:1-4).

We will discuss Daniel's vision later in Revelation 12. Since that chapter tells about Michael fighting for the Jewish people, it seems that Revelation 12 is the prophetic fulfillment of Daniel's apocalyptic vision. Jesus also spoke of this time when the disciples asked Him about signs of His coming and the end of the age. His complete answer is recorded for us in Matthew 24. Jesus mentions events that will happen and says: *"All these are the beginning of sorrows"* (Matt. 24:8). He then says there will be further, more intense sufferings and adds:

> *For then there will be great tribulation, such as has not been seen since the beginning of the world until this time, no, nor ever shall be. And unless those days were short-ened, no flesh would be saved; but for the elect's sake, those days will be shortened* (Matthew 24:21-22).

In our passage from Revelation 7, the elder provides further infor-mation about the great multitude. He tells John that they have washed their robes and made them white in the blood of the Lamb. Now we know that we can't wash a garment in blood to make it white. It will be red. So obviously John is speaking figuratively. He means, of course, that it is the blood of Jesus that cleanses us from all the stains and spots of sin. As we have mentioned, the color white symbolizes moral purity and cleanliness. The white robe clearly represents the "Garment of Sal-vation" or "Robe of Righteousness" of Jesus Himself that is credited to us.

In his wonderful chapter on the good news of salvation, Isaiah wrote:

> *I will greatly rejoice in the LORD, my soul shall be joyful in my God; for He has clothed me with the garments of salvation, He has covered me with the robe of righteous-ness, as a bridegroom decks himself with ornaments, and as a bride adorns herself with her jewels. For as the earth brings forth its bud, as the garden causes the things that are sown in it to spring forth, so the Lord GOD will cause righteousness and praise to spring forth before all the nations* (Isaiah 61:10-11).

Because God is a holy God, our sins separate us from Him. Because He is a just God, He must judge our sins. Because He is a God of love, He doesn't want us to pay the judgment ourselves. Because He is a good God, He came to Earth and paid the penalty for us. This is the central theme throughout the entire Bible from Genesis to Revelation. It is the God-ordained concept of an innocent substitutionary sacrifice dying in place of the guilty. In this way, God's judgment of sin can be administered while, at the same time, mercy is provided for the sinner.

When Adam and Eve sinned, God killed an animal and clothed them with garments made from its skin (see Gen. 3:21). From that moment forward, God instituted His requirement of blood-atonement for sin. He did not do this because He was an angry, bloodthirsty deity demanding death. He did this because He loves us and wanted to make a way for us to be reconciled to Him.

The pagans' idea of sacrifice is to appease their angry gods. The idea of sacrifice in the Bible is to draw near to God. In Chapter 5, we saw the Hebrew word *korban* which is translated "offering." James had this understanding when he said, *"Draw near to God and He will draw near to you..."* (James 4:8).

The Lord summed up His thinking on this issue in Leviticus:

> *For the life of the flesh is in the blood, and I have given it to you upon the altar to make atonement for your souls; for it is the blood that makes atonement for the soul* (Leviticus 17:11).

The writer of Hebrews alludes to this verse and writes:

> *And according to the law almost all things are purified with blood, and without shedding of blood there is no remission* [of sin] (Hebrews 9:22).

The Lord used the blood of animals to provide atonement in the first part of the Bible. However, these animal sacrifices were insufficient. The blood of bulls and goats could only cover sins; it could not take away sins or cause them to be remembered no more. That is why it was necessary for Jesus to die for our sins. His death and the shedding of His blood served as the-once-and-for-all sacrifice. This was God's plan for humanity before He ever created us.

As Peter explains:

> *...you were not redeemed with corruptible things, like silver or gold, from your aimless conduct received by tradition from your fathers, but with the precious blood of Christ* [Messiah], *as of a lamb without blemish and without spot. He indeed was foreordained before the foundation of the world, but was manifest in these last times for you who through Him believe in God, who raised Him from the dead and gave Him glory, so that your faith and hope are in God* (1 Peter 1:18-21).

John's greeting to the seven congregations mentioned the blood of Christ and gave praise for it:

> *...Him who loved us and washed us from our sins in His own blood, and has made us kings and priests to His God and Father, to Him be glory and dominion forever and ever. Amen* (Revelation 1:5-6).

Because the believers in the great multitude have overcome through the blood of the Lamb and the word of their testimony, they have access to the throne of God where they serve Him day and night. Since there is no night in Heaven, this phrase is used figuratively to mean that they never get tired or need rest as we do in these earthly bodies. Hallelujah!

The elder further adds that they are serving God in His Temple. Both Jewish tradition and the Bible speak of a Temple in Heaven (see Heb. 8-9). While we don't know if there is a literal temple in Heaven at this time, we do know that this is John's way of saying that these redeemed saints are forever in the presence of God. We learn later that when God creates a new Heaven and new Earth there will not be a Temple (see Rev. 21:22).

We further learn that God is dwelling among this great multitude. He is both among them and in them at the same time. This has always been God's desire for His people. We should be able to understand this because human parents are also among and in their children. What greater goal and passion in life could we have than this blessing of God living among us and in us.

The English phrase, "dwelling among them" relates to the tabernacle or tent of meeting, and later the Temple, where God dwelled among the Hebrews. The Hebrew word for "tabernacle" is *mishkan*.[6] It is the place where God would meet with His people (see Exodus 25:8).

In Hebrew, the phrase also means "God's manifested glory." The literal manifested glory of God is in their midst. We see examples of this in the Bible when God appeared to Moses in the burning bush (see Exod. 3:2-6), in the pillar of cloud and the pillar of fire that guided the Hebrews in their Exodus from Egypt (see Exod. 13:21-22), and when God manifested Himself at the tabernacle and the Temple (see Exod. 40:34-38; 1 Kings 8:10).

The Hebrew word that refers to this manifested presence of God is *Sh'khinah*. The glorious awe and wonder and anticipation of standing in the blazing glory and dazzling beauty of God should be our greatest and highest motivation.

While the Islamic view of Heaven or paradise involves sensual pleasure, the Judeo-Christian biblical view centers on the indescribable joy of being forever in the presence of God. There is nothing in this world that can compare to this destiny of God's people. We can endure to the end, even through great tribulation, knowing that we will forever be among and in the manifested presence of God.

The elder comforts John and his readers with the assurance that their suffering and the trials of life are over. He refers to the words of Isaiah from the great chapter about the Servant of God who was given as a light to the Gentiles and who would be God's salvation to the ends of the earth (see Isa. 49:6; Luke 2:29-32).

Using the imagery of a shepherd with his sheep, Isaiah explains:

> *They shall neither hunger nor thirst, neither heat nor sun shall strike them; for He who has mercy on them will lead them, even by the springs of water He will guide them* (Isaiah 49:10).

Jesus is the good shepherd who will forever watch over, protect, provide for, and care for his people like a shepherd does for his sheep. They will forever drink from the fountains of living water. The heartaches, disappointments, burdens, and cares of the world will be no more as God will wipe away every tear from their eyes. Lord may it be soon. Amen!

REVIEW QUESTIONS

1. Write a summary of what you have learned in this lesson. Write the summary in clear, concise words as if you were going to present it to another person.

2. Write an explanation of how you can apply what you have learned in this lesson to your life.

3. Share what you have learned with your family, friends, and members of your study group.

ENDNOTES

1. Abraham Joshua Heschel, *God in Search of Man: A Philosophy of Judaism*, (New York: Farrar, Straus and Giroux, 1976), 383.

2. Wording and spelling of this prayer varies slightly from source to source. For your reference: *Hebrew for Christians*, "Netilat Yadayim—Handwashing Blessing," http://www.hebrew4christians.com/Blessings/Daily_Blessings/Upon_Bathing/upon_bathing.html (accessed May 5, 2011).

3. Ibid.

4. Heschel, 311.

5. Biblesoft's New Exhaustive Strong's Numbers and Concordance with Expanded Greek-Hebrew Dictionary. CD-ROM. Biblesoft, Inc. and International Bible Translators, Inc. (1994, 2003, 2006) s.v. "optanomai," (N.T. 3700).

6. Biblesoft's New Exhaustive Strong's, s.v. "mishkan," (O.T. 4908).

Chapter 8

Opening the Seventh Seal

Revelation Review

AS we have learned, the exalted Son of Man is both the Lamb of God and the Lion of the Tribe of Judah. Because of His perfect obedience to His Father to live a sinless life and die for our sins, He alone is the worthy Redeemer who is able to open the seven-sealed scroll. This scroll contains the prophecies for the last days leading to the return of Jesus to Earth.

The Lord opens the seven-sealed scroll to reveal horrific end-time events. God's just judgments are not against His people but against those who oppose Him. In fact, the judgments are God's answer to the prayers of His people for God to avenge them. While this is a time of doom and gloom for unbelievers, it is the greatest opportunity in all of history for God's people to witness to their faith in the One True God and His Messiah, Jesus of Nazareth.

To this point, God has opened the first six seals. The seventh seal is the seven trumpet-shofar judgments and the seventh trumpet-shofar is the seven bowl judgments. Whereas the first six seals are somewhat general, the seventh seal releases the trumpet-shofar and bowl judgments, which are much more specific and severe.

Before opening the seventh seal, God places a mark or seal of protection on His own. While God's people are protected from His wrath, which is now going to be revealed, they are persecuted by those who hate God.

In his apocalyptic vision, John fast forwards to the end of this time of tribulation and sees the people of God before the throne of God. They are the victors who overcame the evil one by the blood of the Lamb and the word of their testimony (see Rev. 12:11). With this assurance of victory for His people, the Lord now opens the seventh seal.

OPENING THE SEVENTH SEAL
(REVELATION 8-9)

Revelation 8—The First Four Trumpet-Shofar Judgments

The contents of the seventh seal are explained in Revelation chapters 8 and 9. These chapters advance the chronology of events. Chapters 10 and 11 are informational chapters with the last part of chapter 11 sounding the seventh trumpet-shofar. Chapters 12 through 15 provide more information. The content of the seventh trumpet-shofar is the bowl judgment explained in chapter 16. This means that the seventh seal provides the information for the rest of the tribulation up to and including the appearing of the Lord in Revelation 19.

The story of the Book of Revelation actually ends at the end of Revelation chapter 11. The rest is what I call the "instant replay" of John's vision in which he adds more details to what he has already seen. This insight is a major breakthrough in understanding the Book of Revelation. Let's now see what the future holds for those who oppose God and His people.

Preparing to Open the Seventh Seal (verses 1-6)

When the Lord opens the seventh seal, all the glorious worship and praise of Heaven stops. What a contrast: from the loudest and deepest worship and highest praise, the throne room of God is now silent. Can you image silence in Heaven for thirty minutes? It is like all of the heavenly hosts are holding their breath waiting for the Lord to reveal its contents. We might say that this is the "lull before the storm."

There are occasions when the manifested presence of God is so holy, the only response is silence. In the Hebrew Bible we learn that there are times when God does something so dramatic, His people need to be silent. Zechariah writes: *"Be silent, all flesh, before the LORD, for He is aroused from His holy habitation!"* (Zech. 2:13). Habakkuk cautions: *"But the LORD is in His holy temple. Let all the earth keep silence before Him"* (Hab. 2:20).

John makes note of the Jewish tradition of his time that seven specific archangels stand before the presence of God to do His bidding. In the intertestamental book of Tobit, the angel says:

> I am Raphael, one of the seven holy angels, which present the prayers of the saints, and which go in and out before the glory of the Holy One.[1]

In Enoch 20:2-8 their names are given as Uriel, Raphael, Raguel, Michael, Saraqael, Gabriel, and Remiel.

The archangels were given seven trumpets or shofars. The shofar was blown for many reasons, one of which was to announce the judgments of God. There are numerous places in the Hebrew Bible that mention this use of the shofar.

For example Joel reads:

> *Blow the trumpet* [shofar] *in Zion, and sound an alarm in My holy mountain! Let all the inhabitants of the land*

tremble; for the day of the LORD is coming, for it is at hand (Joel 2:1).

If you would like information on the use of the shofar in the Bible, you may order my publication, *The Shofar: Ancient Sounds of the Messiah.*[2]

Before the archangels blow the shofars, John sees another angel standing at the altar with a golden censer. John specifically mentions that this angel has much incense. John explains using imagery from the tabernacle and later the Temple that the angel sprinkles the incense over the hot coals of the altar causing the smoke of the incense to billow up in the presence of God.

We learn in the Book of Exodus that the priests offered incense before the Lord every morning and every evening:

> *Aaron shall burn on it* [the incense altar] *sweet incense every morning; when he tends the lamps, he shall burn incense on it. And when Aaron lights the lamps at twilight, he shall burn incense on it, a perpetual incense before the LORD throughout your generations* (Exodus 30:7-8).

In addition to this action, once a year, the high priest would take blood from the brazen altar in the courtyard and smear it on the horns of the incense altar. He would then sprinkle the incense on the hot coals. As the sweet incense filled the room, the high priest would enter the holy of holies directly into the presence of God. Leviticus reads:

> *Then he* [Aaron] *should take a censer full of burning coals of fire from the altar before the LORD, with his hands full of sweet incense beaten fine, and bring it inside the veil. And he shall put the incense on the fire before the LORD, that the cloud of incense may cover the mercy seat that is on the Testimony* [Ark of the Covenant], *lest he die* (Leviticus 16:12-13).

We learn in the Book of Psalms that incense offered before God is the biblical symbol of the prayers of God's people. Psalm 141:2 reads: *"Let my prayer be set before You as incense, the lifting up of my hands as the evening sacrifice."* When John says the angel has much incense, his contemporary readers would have understood him to mean that God's people have offered many prayers for justice against those who have persecuted them.

When the angel throws the fire-incense to the earth, it symbolizes God answering the prayers of His people. God's response to their prayers results in a great shaking on the earth which John describes as noises, thunderings, lightnings, and an earthquake. John describes similar "shakings" on the earth at the seventh trumpet-shofar (see Rev. 11:19) and the seventh bowl judgment (see Rev. 16:18). It is important to understand that these are also our prayers that God is answering.

The First Four Trumpet-Shofar Judgments (verses 7-12)

In answer to the prayers of His people, God releases seven trumpet-shofar judgments on the earth. In the final trumpet-shofar described in chapter 16, God further releases seven bowl judgments.

In the previous chapter we learned that the Lord restrained the four angels from releasing God's judgments on the earth's vegetation and water until He sealed His people for protection against these judgments. Now that this has been accomplished, the Lord opens the seventh seal.

The first four of these trumpet-shofar judgments are against the earth's natural resources. In each judgment, a third of the natural resources are devastated. The last three are spiritual judgments through demonic activities.

Before considering these judgments, it is important to understand their purpose. They are God's judgments against the gods of the world system that the people worship. They are not against the people themselves, although it is the people who suffer. The reason God sends these judgments is to show the world that He is the One True God and to bring people to repentance.

This is what the Lord did when He sent the plagues in Egypt. The plagues were not against Pharaoh and the Egyptian people but against the gods that Pharaoh and the people worshiped. Yet, it was the people who suffered because they worshiped these false gods. The list below shows the gods that the Egyptians worshiped and the plagues that the One True God sent against each of them to show His sovereignty and superiority and to warn Pharaoh to repent.

Egyptian Deities	God's Judgment Plague
Osiris—god of the Nile	the Nile turned to blood
Heqt—frog goddess	frogs covered the land
Seb—Earth god	dust turned to lice
Scarabus—a flying bug	swarms of flies
Apis—bull god	death to livestock
Neit—god of health	boils and sores
Shu—god of nature	hail and fire
Serapia—god of locusts	locusts eat what remains
Ra—the sun god	darkness over the land
Pharaoh—incarnation of Ra	death of firstborn

The First Trumpet-Shofar (verse 7)

While we don't fully understand the nature of these judgments, when John says he sees something thrown from Heaven to Earth, this wording means that the judgments are God's answer to the prayers of His people. Since we don't fully understand these judgments, any comments would only be opinions. Our studied views are interesting and can be clarifying, but they are not authoritative.

This first judgment of hail and fire mixed with blood is said to be thrown to the earth. This is God's judgment on the earth's vegetation. The result is that one-third of the trees and all green grass are burned up. Some translations add that one-third of the earth is burned up. With the Weather Channel available to us today we certainly can understand the devastation caused by hail and fire and tornadoes and lightning.

This judgment is similar to the seventh plague in Egypt:

> *So there was hail, and fire mingled with the hail, so very heavy that there was none like it in all the land of Egypt since it became a nation. And the hail struck throughout the whole land of Egypt, all that was in the field, both man and beast; and the hail struck every herb of the field and broke every tree of the field* (Exodus 9:24-25).

In describing the day of God's judgments on the earth, Joel laments:

> *O LORD, to You I cry out; for fire has devoured the open pastures, and a flame has burned all the trees of the field* (Joel 1:19).

God made an interesting statement to Job when He was rebuking him. The Lord asked Job the following questions:

Have you entered the treasury of snow, or have you seen the treasury of hail, which I have reserved for the time of trouble, for the day of battle and war? (Job 38:22-23).

The Second Trumpet-Shofar (verses 8-9)

In this second judgment, John describes a great mountain burning with fire thrown into the sea. The result is that one-third of the sea becomes blood, a third of everything in the sea dies, and a third of oceangoing vessels are destroyed.

All of these judgments may show God doing something supernatural He has never done before or God disrupting the normal order of His creation. We know in the Bible and in history that God has worked through nature to accomplish His purposes. In fact, most great battles in history were won due to the weather, not because of superior armaments—and we know who is in charge of the weather.

God may be originating something new in these judgments or John could be describing volcanic eruptions from the bottom of the ocean floor. This could also be the eruption of existing dormant volcanoes. As we know, seismic activity on a large scale can cause great upheavals in the ocean such as the forming of volcanoes, earthquakes, and tsunamis. This could certainly cause the results John describes. Such natural phenomena happen all the time, just not on this scale.

This judgment reminds us of the first plague God sent in Egypt against Osiris, the god of the Nile. God turned the Nile River into blood, killing the fish in the Nile and making the Nile undrinkable.

Exodus reads:

Then the LORD spoke to Moses, "Say to Aaron, 'Take your rod and stretch out your hand over the waters of Egypt, over their streams, over their rivers, over their ponds, and over all their pools of water, that they may become blood. And there shall be blood throughout all the land of Egypt, both in buckets of wood and pitchers of stone."' And Moses and Aaron did so, just as the LORD commanded. So he lifted up the rod and struck the waters that were in the river, in the sight of Pharaoh and in the sight of his servants. And all the waters that were in the river were turned to blood. The fish that were in the river died, the river stank, and the Egyptians could not drink the water of the river. So there was blood throughout all the land of Egypt (Exodus 7:19-21).

The Third Trumpet-Shofar (verses 10-11)

Whereas the second trumpet-shofar judgment is on salt water, this third trumpet-shofar devastates one-third of the earth's fresh water. In John's vision he sees a phenomenon that he describes as a great burning star falling from Heaven into the rivers and fresh water sources. He says the name of the star is Wormwood. Whether this is a supernatural phenomenon or natural disruption from God, the judgment makes the waters bitter and poisonous to drink.

The word translated "wormwood" actually indicates bitterness.[3] It is a plant which has a very bitter taste. If a person ingested very much of the oil from the plant, they could die from the poison that is in the plant. Because of its bitter taste and potential as a deadly poison, people in the Bible spoke of wormwood as something bad, a symbol of God's judgment or their suffering.

For example in Proverbs, the temptations of an immoral woman are likened to wormwood. On the surface, she is sweet but if one "drinks" of her cup of sin, the supposed sweetness turns to wormwood:

For the lips of an immoral woman drip honey, and her mouth is smoother than oil; but in the end she is bitter as wormwood... (Proverbs 5:3-4).

Because God's people turned away from Him, the Lord told Jeremiah that He would give them wormwood as a judgment:

> *Therefore thus says the LORD of hosts, the God of Israel:*
> *"Behold, I will feed them, this people, with wormwood,*
> *and give them water of gall* [poisonous water] *to drink"*
> (Jeremiah 9:15; see Jeremiah 23:15).

When Jeremiah complained to the Lord about his ridicule and suffering as God's prophet, he said:

> *I have become the ridicule of all my people—their taunting song all the day. He has filled me with bitterness, He has made me drink wormwood* (Lamentations 3:14-15).

The Fourth Trumpet-Shofar (verse 12)

While the first three trumpet-shofar judgments were directed at the earth, the fourth judgment is seen as God's sovereignty over the lights He placed in the sky. As a manifestation of His sovereign power over His creation, God darkens the sun, the moon, and the stars for a third of the day and night. This darkness could be the result of the three previous judgments; it could also be the result of a solar or lunar eclipse; or it might indicate that God is orchestrating it supernaturally. It really doesn't matter how God does this, the results are the same.

God darkened the sun in the ninth plague against Egypt. The Egyptians worshiped the sun and Pharaoh was thought to be the incarnation of Ra, the sun god. The One True God demonstrated His sovereign superiority over the Egyptian deity by darkening the sun. It was so completely dark that the people could not see anything. God's judgment was not against His own people, so they had light.

Exodus reads:

> *Then the LORD said to Moses, "Stretch out your hand toward heaven, that there may be darkness over the land of Egypt, darkness which may even be felt." So Moses stretched out his hand toward heaven, and there was thick darkness in all the land of Egypt three days. They did not see one another; nor did anyone rise from his place for three days. But all the children of Israel had light in their dwellings* (Exodus 10:21-23).

The prophets spoke of the day of the Lord when God would judge the world by darkening the lights in the sky. Isaiah wrote:

> *Behold, the day of the LORD comes, cruel, with both wrath and fierce anger, to lay the land desolate; and He will destroy its sinners from it. For the stars of heaven and the constellations will not give their light; the sun will be darkened it its going forth, and the moon will not cause its light to shine* (Isaiah 13:9-10).

Joel spoke about these judgments in the day of the Lord:

> *The earth quakes before them, the heavens tremble; the sun and moon grow dark, and the stars diminish their brightness* (Joel 2:10).

Amos explained:

> *Woe to you who desire the day of the LORD! For what good is the day of the LORD to you? It will be darkness, and not light* (Amos 5:18).

In His summary prophecy of the endtimes, Jesus spoke of these signs in the heavens happening just prior to His coming:

Immediately after the tribulation of those days the sun will be darkened, and the moon will not give its light; the stars will fall from heaven, and the powers of the heavens will be shaken. Then the sign of the Son of Man will appear in heaven, and then all the tribes of the earth will mourn, and they will see the Son of Man coming on the clouds of heaven with power and great glory (Matthew 24:29-30).

Luke recorded similar words from Jesus:

And there will be signs in the sun, in the moon, and in the stars; and on the earth distress of nations, with perplexity, the sea and the waves roaring; men's hearts failing them from fear and the expectation of those things which are coming on the earth, for the powers of the heavens will be shaken. Then they will see the Son of Man coming in a cloud with power and great glory. Now when these things begin to happen, look up and lift up your heads, because your redemption draws near (Luke 21:25-28).

"Woe, Woe, Woe" (verse 13)

We would think that all of this clear demonstration of the sovereignty and supremacy of the One True God would cause people to repent of their sins and turn to Him. Unfortunately it doesn't. It is truly difficult for us to understand the hardness of people's hearts against God. They would rather curse God and die than acknowledge Him and repent.

Once again, we turn to Pharaoh as an example. When God sent the first plague, how did Pharaoh respond? Instead of repenting, Exodus says, *"And Pharaoh's heart grew hard, and he did not heed them, as the LORD had said"* (Exod. 7:13).

He responded in the same way after the second plague: *"But when Pharaoh saw that there was relief, he hardened his heart and did not heed them, as the LORD had said"* (Exod. 8:15).

After the third plague, even Pharaoh's magicians understood that the One True God was sending the plagues. It didn't matter to Pharaoh.

> *Then the magicians said to Pharaoh, "This is the finger of God." But Pharaoh's heart grew hard, and he did not heed them, just as the LORD had said* (Exodus 8:19).

Nothing changed after the fourth plague: *"But Pharaoh hardened his heart at this time also; neither would he let the people go"* (Exod. 8:32). Pharaoh responded the same way after each plague (see Exod. 9:7,12,35; 10:20,27; 11:9-10).

We don't normally think of these plagues as a means of God showing His mercy. However, God could have sent one plague and that would have been enough. He could have judged them immediately. In fact, at Passover, the Jewish people sing a special song entitled, *Dayenu,* which means "it would have been enough."[4] But in His mercy, God exposed the hardness of Pharaoh's heart by sending a succession of plagues until it was clear that Pharaoh would never repent.

As we will see in the following woes, the people experiencing these "Day of the Lord" judgments respond in the same way as Pharaoh. In view of God's continuing to show mercy by giving people the opportunity to repent, no one can say His judgments are unjust. He sends more judgments until it is clear the people will not repent. It is at this time, that Jesus returns to bring the final judgment against the ungodly.

REVELATION 9—THE FIFTH AND
SIXTH TRUMPET-SHOFAR JUDGMENTS

In view of the hardness of the people's hearts, God announces three additional judgments called "woes." These three woes are the fifth, sixth, and seventh trumpet-shofar judgments (the seventh trumpet-shofar judgment being the seven bowl judgments).

Since these woes involve releasing demonic activity, they are directed against those who oppose God. They are not against God's own people. God has already put the seal of protection on those who are His. Once again, we remind ourselves that these judgments are God's answer to the prayers of His people for justice. This is the wrath of God against an unrepentant world.

The Fifth Trumpet-Shofar (verses 1-12)

In the first woe, John gives a vivid description of frightening tormenters that inflict terrible suffering on those who have the Mark of the Beast. Using apocalyptic language he sees a star that has fallen from Heaven to Earth with the key to the bottomless pit. Since this is apocalyptic symbolism, we have to do our best to correctly interpret the meaning of John's words.

First of all, John does not literally mean a star. He is talking about an angel. There are several reasons why we should think this is an angel. In the Book of Job angels are called stars. God rebuked Job and said that angels sing His praises. God also refers to them as the "sons of God" in that He created them. God speaks of a heavenly praise service, *"When the morning stars sang together, and all the sons of God shouted for joy..."* (Job 38:7). This is Hebrew parallelism in which both the morning stars and the sons of God are the same company of angels.

Also, in Revelation 20, John says that he saw an angel coming down from Heaven with the key to the bottomless pit:

> *Then I saw an angel coming down from heaven, having the key to the bottomless pit and a great chain in his hand* (Revelation 20:1).

When John says that the angel has the key to the bottomless pit, he means that God has given the angel the authority and permission to release those held in the bottomless pit. So what is the bottomless pit? Who is held in it? And why is God releasing them?

In the Bible, the phrase "bottomless pit" refers to the abode of demons. To the best of our understanding, these are spirit beings that followed lucifer in his rebellion against God. They are so evil God has bound them or "chained them" in the bottomless pit until this time when He releases them as part of His "Day of the Lord" judgments.

Peter referred to these demons and said:

> *...God did not spare the angels who sinned, but cast them down to hell* [Tartarus, an abyss[5] or bottomless pit]*, and delivered them into chains of darkness, to be reserved for judgment...* (2 Peter 2:4).

Jude adds:

> *And the angels who did not keep their proper domain, but left their own abode, He has reserved in everlasting chains under darkness for the judgment of the great day* (Jude 6).

When Jesus was ministering in the area of the Gadarenes (the modern-day Golan Heights) He encountered a man who was demon-possessed. When Jesus confronted the demons, *"they begged Him that He would not command them to go out into the abyss* [bottomless pit]" (Luke 8:31). The Lord actually honored their request and sent them into a herd of swine (pigs). You recall from the story that when the demons entered the swine, the animals went crazy and ran off the cliff into the Sea of Galilee.

When the angel opens the bottomless pit, a tremendous amount of smoke is released into the air. There is so much smoke that everything turns dark. Then out of the smoke, John sees locusts.

The very mention of the word *locust* was frightening to John's contemporary readers. An invasion of locusts was a common plague in the world of the Bible. John's readers knew that a swarm of locusts could consist of millions of hungry, winged creatures that darken the sky due to their great numbers. While their lifespan and the harvest season are only five months, locusts can strip the land of all the grass, trees, and crops, leaving behind them total devastation. With their massive numbers, they can devour the land in a very short period of time and move on to destroy another location.

We recall that the Lord used locusts in His eighth plague against Pharaoh. Exodus reads:

> *For they covered the face of the whole earth, so that the land was darkened; and they ate every herb of the land and all the fruit of the trees which the hail had left. So there remained nothing green on the trees or on the plants of the field throughout all the land of Egypt* (Exodus 10:15).

One of the most devastating locust plagues took place in the heart of the American breadbasket in 1875. In an article entitled, "When the Skies Turned to Black," Hearthstone Legacy Publications gives the following report.

While the agricultural production of the states of Nebraska, Iowa, and Kansas has helped feed the world, a plague of locusts stripped the land leaving it barren. The states of Missouri and Minnesota were also devastated. It was a swarm of Rocky Mountain locusts estimated to number in the trillions. They came out of nowhere and within hours devoured every crop in their pathway. Observers at that time estimated that the swarm was 1,800 miles long (yes, that number is correct) and 110 miles wide. Eyewitnesses say that the heavens were darkened. The locusts vanished as quickly as they appeared, leaving the country bare of vegetation. (www.hearthstonelegacy.com/ when the skies turned to black the locust plague of 1875.)

The locusts in Revelation are not ordinary locusts. John's description of them is terrifying. The prophet Joel compares an invading army to a swarm of locusts and gives a description similar to John's (see Joel 2:4-5). The point of John's description is for his readers to understand that, like locusts, this is a powerful swarm, or army, which cannot be stopped.

While literal locusts eat everything in their way, these locusts do not eat the crops. They torment people, specifically people who have taken the Mark of the Beast. John likens the pain they inflict to that of the sting of a scorpion. While the sting of a scorpion is extremely painful, it is not normally fatal.

Likewise, those tormented by these locusts suffer great pain for five months. They are in such anguish that they try to kill themselves but are restrained from doing so. John adds that the locusts are ruled over by an angel who is king of the bottomless pit. His *"name in Hebrew is Abaddon, but in Greek he has the name Apollyon"* (Rev. 9:11). Both of these words have the same meaning of "destroyer."[6]

We should be able to understand by all that John says about these locusts are they are not literal locusts but a demonic army released by God as a judgment on those who oppose Him. John gives us a big clue when he says they have a king over them because literal locusts don't have a king, according to Proverbs 30:27, which says, *"The locusts have no king; yet they all advance in ranks."* The fallen angel who is king of the bottomless pit is most likely satan.

John's readers would have also been familiar with the imagery of smoke coming out of the bottomless pit. When we discussed the Lord's letter to the congregation at Laodicea in Volume 1, I pointed out that Laodicea, Colosse, and Hierapolis were a tri-city area located within a few miles of each other.

Hierapolis was the city with the hot mineral springs that constantly bubbled at the top like we see at Yellowstone National Park. These springs gave the appearance of a "lake of fire" that could erupt at any moment, much like Old Faithful, the geyser at Yellowstone that erupts like clockwork to the amazement and amusement of tourists.

The chief deity of Hierapolis was the Greek god Apollo, which I discussed in the chapter about Thyatira. There was a temple to Apollo and underneath this temple was a deep cave which the people believed to be the home of Hades (Greek) or Pluto (Roman). In Greek mythology, Hades or Pluto was the god of the underworld or god of the dead. Since the cave was believed to be the home of Pluto, it was called "the Plutonium."

In his excellent publication, *Understanding the Revelation*, scholar and archeologist Jim Fleming gives the following fascinating explanation. There was an entrance from the temple into the Plutonium which emitted a dense fog of poisonous gas from the cave. The priest of Pluto knew how far down into the cave they could go before inhaling the gas. As a way of influencing and controlling the people, the priests would take an animal with them into the cave to sacrifice to Pluto. Of course, the animal did not know how far down to go before inhaling the gas. It would die but the priests would live. As you can imagine, this was most impressive to a superstitious people who had a primitive understanding of the earth's natural resources.

When John wrote about seeing great fiery smoke coming out of the bottomless pit with locusts released to torment the people, they understood what he meant. The people lived in constant fear of the demonic spirits of the underworld. The imagery of steaming hot springs flowing out of caves, lakes of fire, earthquakes, and volcanoes spewing out smoke and fire was all around them.

It is ironic that the very people these demons are attacking in Revelation 9 are the ones who took the Mark of the Beast. They are the ones who sold their souls to satan. These demons are tormenting their own followers. And that is the way satan operates. While he appears as an angel of light (see 2 Cor. 11:14), his destructive nature, and that of his demonic army, destroys his own people. Those who take the Mark of the Beast thinking they will escape persecution will, in the end, be tormented and killed by the evil ones they thought would later protect them from harm. What a tragic miscalculation!

John notes that this is the first woe but two more are coming. Yet, no matter how many woes God sends, like Pharaoh, the people still refuse to repent.

The Sixth Trumpet-Shofar (verses 13-21)

Before John can finish contemplating the horrors of the first woe, he hears a voice from the four horns of the altar calling the sixth angel to sound the trumpet-shofar for the second woe. In Revelation 6:9-11 we learned that those who gave their lives for their faith were seen under the altar crying out for God to avenge their deaths. They are said to be "under the altar" because when the sacrifices were made at the tabernacle and Temple, the blood of the sacrifices poured out under the altar. The Lord told them to wait a little while and their prayers would be answered.

In Revelation 8:3-6 an angel presented the prayers of these faithful to the Lord as it was time for God to answer them. As we have been reminded, the judgments are God's answer to the prayers of His people. All true believers cry out to God to vindicate their lives, judge evil, and establish righteousness on the earth. While God has answered these prayers in part throughout history, these judgments are the final answer to our prayers. While we are saddened at the suffering brought about by the judgments, we rejoice in the final destruction of evil.

The voice of the angel at the altar now instructs the sixth angel to give the signal for the sixth trumpet-shofar judgment. The sixth angel is told to release the four angels who are bound at the Euphrates River. Who are these four angels and why the Euphrates River?

John is made to understand that God has bound these angels for a specific time in history until He is ready to release them. In the Bible, the angels who serve God are never bound, only fallen angels (demons) who followed lucifer in his rebellion against God. While God has allowed many of these demons the freedom to be active in our world, He has restrained others.

To the best of our understanding, these four angels are powerful demons that God has kept bound throughout history just as He had bound the demonic spirits in the bottomless pit. Since it is time for God to use them for His purposes, He releases them to attack those who oppose Him. Again we see the irony: the people the demons attack are the people who unwittingly serve them.

John informs us that these powerful demonic spirits are bound at the Euphrates River. Why the Euphrates River? There are several reasons. In the ancient world, the Euphrates River was the natural boundary separating the East from the West. When the invading armies from the East attacked the Western nations, they had to cross the Euphrates River. The Assyrians, Babylonians, Persians, and Medes all came from the East. The Euphrates River was also the eastern boundary of the Roman Empire. The powerful Parthian army was on the other side ready to attack Rome.

There was also a spiritual connection to the Euphrates River as it was the eastern boundary of the land God promised to Abraham and his descendants through Isaac and Jacob (see Gen. 15:18). In Bible times, God's people considered the nations to the east of the Euphrates to be pagans who worshiped demons. For example, Babylon was where Nimrod attempted to establish the first organized religion against God (see Gen. 11:1-9). The Babylonian religion was spread to future empires including Rome. It became the "Mother Religion" of all religions that were contrary to the worship of the One True God. So the Euphrates was both a natural and spiritual barrier separating God's people from those opposed to God.

These four demonic spirits are so powerful they are able to send forth a great army to attack those who had the Mark of the Beast. John says their number is 200 million. This is the ultimate in spiritual warfare. Whether this number is literal or an apocalyptic way of saying "more than we can number" their evil, destructive nature causes the death of one-third of all human life.

Scholars have different views about the nature of this great army. Some believe it to be a literal army representing the first phase of the last great battle which is further described in Revelation 16:12-16. Others believe, due to the size and description of this army, that John is seeing an innumerable company of demonic spirits. Regardless, the devastation is the same—a third of humanity is killed by the fire, smoke, and brimstone coming out of the demon's mouths. John could be describing modern nuclear warfare as some believe, or spiritual manifestations of demonic power, or both.

Now any reasonable person would think that people who survived this horror would turn to God. But unfortunately, they do not. There is nothing rational or logical about sin. It is willful rebellion against God. John says they do not repent of their worship of demons and idols, their murders, their sorceries, their sexual immorality, or their thefts. Wow—hard to believe! Like Pharaoh, they harden their hearts against God.

It is interesting that John mentions "sorceries" (see Rev. 9:21). This English word is translated from the Greek word *"pharmakeia."*[7] You can probably recognize the English words that are derived from *"pharmakeia."* Yes, they are the words pharmacy or pharmaceutical. Now what do we get at the pharmacy? We get drugs. The occult uses drugs to alter the minds of their followers so they can control them.

What we see here is a description of a world of people who have sold their souls to the devil, cannot make sound decisions due to the influence of drugs, and have no moral constraints. They are totally controlled by evil spirits. While God in His mercy has made every effort to bring these people to repentance, they continue to refuse to acknowledge and submit to Him. Since they will not accept redemption, what choice does a just God have but to bring further judgment?

REVIEW QUESTIONS

1. Write a summary of what you have learned in this lesson. Write the summary in clear, concise words as if you were going to present it to another person.

2. Write an explanation of how you can apply what you have learned in this lesson to your life.

3. Share what you have learned with your family, friends, and members of your study group.

ENDNOTES

1. The Book of Tobit 12:15; www.sacredtexts.com; accessed December 7, 2011.

2. Available at my online bookstore at www.rbooker.com.

3. Biblesoft's New Exhaustive Strong's Numbers and Concordance with Expanded Greek-Hebrew Dictionary. CD-ROM. Biblesoft, Inc. and International Bible Translators, Inc. (1994, 2003, 2006) s.v. "apsinthos," (N.T. 894).

4. Chayem B. Alevsky, "Dayenu: 'It would have been sufficient,'" Chabad.org, http://www.chabad.org/multimedia/media_cdo/aid/255530/jewish/Dayenu.htm (accessed May 13, 2011).

5. Biblesoft's New Exhaustive Strong's, s.v. "tartaroo," (N.T. 5020) and *Blue Letter Bible*, Dictionary and Word Search for *"tartaroō"* (Strong's 5020), 1996-2011, < http:// www.blueletterbible.org/lang/

lexicon/lexicon.cfm?
Strongs=G5020&t=KJV > (accessed May 11, 2011).

6. Biblesoft's New Exhaustive Strong's, s.v. "Abaddon," and s.v., "Apolluon," (N.T. 3 and N.T. 623).

7. Biblesoft's New Exhaustive Strong's, s.v. "pharmakeus," (N.T. 5332).

Chapter 9

The Mighty Angel and the Little Book

REVELATION REVIEW

THE God of Abraham, Isaac, and Jacob is a God of love and mercy. Since humans are created in God's image, we also have these attributes. However, because of our fallen, sinful nature, these divine qualities in us are overshadowed by our self-centeredness. Therefore, when we do manifest godly qualities, they are greatly diminished by our sinful tendencies.

Unlike us, God is perfect in His person and in all His ways. This means He is holy. While God wants to manifest His love and mercy toward us, He is bound by His own perfection. He must be true to Himself. This means that if we will not receive His love and mercy, God must judge us out of His holy justice.

We clearly see God doing this in the Book of Revelation. God's love and mercy mark those who are His to protect them against His holy wrath while His justice is manifested toward those who oppose Him. Therefore, when God's own people cry out for justice, God answers them by releasing the judgments described in the Book of Revelation.

As we continue to study these terrible judgments, let not our hearts be troubled. I have stated numerous times that these judgments are not against God's people. God is judging the godless world system. He is bringing it to an end. The kingdoms of this world are becoming the kingdoms of our Lord and of His Messiah (see Rev. 11:15).

While our faith will soon be tested, victory is certain. We face the future with faith, not fear; with hope, not despair; and with joyous expectation of the good that God has promised. We will overcome by the blood of the Lamb and the word of our testimony (see Rev. 12:11). Yes, we grieve over human suffering, but we rejoice in the sure knowledge that God's righteousness and His people will prevail.

We have seen God's judgments manifested in the opening of the seven seals. The seventh seal opens the seven trumpet-shofar judgments. The seventh trumpet-shofar judgment will open the seven bowl judgments. But before God allows the seventh trumpet-shofar to sound, He gives John further information regarding events to take place on the earth.

This means that Revelation chapter ten is an informational chapter. It does not seem to advance the story but is a "divine pause" before God sends more judgments. The seventh angel sounds the seventh trumpet-shofar judgment which is recorded in Revelation 11:15. However, John is not given the revelation of what the judgment is until Revelation 16, which describes the seven bowl judgments.

It seems, therefore, that in chapters 10-15, John is given more information so that he can have a fuller understanding of events happening on the earth. Then in chapter 16, the chronology of events continues with the revelation of the seven bowl judgments. Let's now join John in his vision of a mighty angel who has a little book in his hand.

The Mighty Angel and the Little Book
(Revelation 10)

The Mighty Angel and the Little Book (verses 1-7)

As of the writing of this book, I can say that I have, from time to time, seen a glimpse of the glory of God. But I am not aware that I have ever seen an angel. I fully expect to see angels in the days ahead as God allows them to be more visibly active in their service to Him and to God's people.

The angel John sees is not an ordinary angel. It is a mighty angel. John says that it is *"another mighty angel,"* meaning that he has seen an angel like this one earlier in his vision. He may be referring to the *"strong angel"* he mentioned in Revelation 5:2. That angel asked the question to all of Heaven, *"Who is worthy to open the scroll and to loose its seals?"* The same Greek word, *ischuros,* is translated as "mighty" and "strong"[1] in English. Both are angels of great rank and power.

The Lord sends this second mighty angel with a message for John which he records in Revelation 10. Three times John mentions that the angel has one foot on the sea and the other on the land (see Rev. 10:2,5,8). The fact that this angel has one foot on the sea and another on the land is John's way of saying that the angel has a message for the whole world. This description of how the angel is standing is a clear and powerful statement that *"The earth is the LORD's and all its fullness, the world and those who dwell therein"* (Ps. 24:1).

The description of the angel is not as important as the function he serves. Yet, the description is breathtaking. I am sure that seeing an ordinary angel is overwhelming. But seeing an angel like this one would certainly be a defining moment in life, one which none of us would ever forget.

This may be the same angel Daniel saw when God gave him a vision of the endtimes. Daniel described that angel with these words:

His body was like beryl, his face like the appearance of lighting, his eyes like torches of fire, his arms and feet like burnished bronze in color, and the sound of his words like the voice of a multitude (Daniel 10:6).

No wonder the vision of this mighty angel so overwhelmed Daniel that he was not able to stand in his presence (see Dan. 10:8-9). Anyone who has had an overwhelming experience with the manifested presence of the Holy Spirit can understand this.

The angel in John's vision has a little book in his hand. That the book is open suggests that God is going to reveal its contents. When the angel gives a mighty shout, John likens his voice to that of a roaring lion. When a lion roars, everyone nearby is alerted. Similarly, the sound of the angel's awesome voice is the signal for the contents of the seventh trumpet-shofar judgment to be revealed to John.

John hears seven thunders uttering their voices. John doesn't literally mean the physical phenomenon of thunder. It is his apocalyptic way of describing heavenly voices that are as loud as thunder. The voices reveal the contents of the seventh trumpet-shofar. As John is about to write down what he hears, another voice from Heaven tells him to seal up, or keep to himself, the words of the seven thunderous voices. In chapter 16, we learn what the seven thunder voices are saying. They proclaim the seven bowl judgments. But for now, God does not want John to reveal their words.

The mighty angel then lifts up his hand to Heaven and swears, or makes an oath, in the name of the One True God that the time for His final judgment has come. God will no longer offer His mercy to those who have opposed Him. Their time to repent is over.

This action of swearing by an oath is mentioned in Leviticus 5:1. There the Lord says that if someone is put under an oath as a witness, they must speak the truth of what they have heard or seen or know to be true. This is the Scripture that the high priest used to coax Jesus to defend Himself just before His crucifixion:

> *But Jesus kept silent. And the high priest answered and said to Him, "I put You under oath by the living God; Tell us if You are the Christ [Messiah], the Son of God!" Jesus said to him, "It is as you said. Nevertheless, I say to you, hereafter you will see the Son of Man sitting at the right hand of the Power, and coming on the clouds of heaven"* (Matthew 26:63-64).

We still follow this custom today when witnesses are sworn in at court. Each witness places his left hand on the Bible and raises his right hand, promising to tell "the whole truth and nothing but the truth, so help me God."

Returning to Daniel, we see a similar exchange between Daniel and the powerful angel talking with him. After the angel gave Daniel prophetic revelation, the angel told Daniel to seal up the vision until the time of the end:

> *But you, Daniel, shut up the words, and seal the book until the time of the end; many shall run to and fro, and knowledge shall increase* (Daniel 12:4).

When asked how long it would be before the prophecies were fulfilled, the angel lifted up his hands to Heaven and swore by Him who lives forever and ever that the end-time events would occur in God's own time. When Daniel inquired further, the angel said to Daniel:

> *...Go your way, Daniel, for the words are closed up and sealed till the time of the end. Many shall be purified, made white, and refined, but the wicked shall do wickedly; and none of the wicked shall understand, but the wise shall understand* (Daniel 12:9-10).

It should seem obvious to us that this final revelation to John is the fulfillment of the words the angel gave to Daniel. The seven-sealed scroll has been opened. All but the last trumpet-shofar have been blown. The contents of the last judgment are sealed for now but will soon be revealed. As Peter wrote: "...The end of all things is at hand..." (1 Pet. 4:7).

The angel then confirms that when the seventh trumpet-shofar sounds, the mystery of God will be finished. While the angel doesn't say what he means by "the mystery of God," he does say God declares it to His servants the prophets. What is the mystery of God? What did God declare to the prophets?

The mystery of God is His divine plan or secret which He is either yet to reveal or which He has already revealed to those who did not fully understand it. It's a mystery. But at some point in God's timing, the mystery will be understood.

The angel says that God has revealed His mystery to His prophets. The angel means the prophets in the Hebrew Bible. The angel is referencing Amos which says, *"Surely the Lord God does nothing, unless He reveals His secret to His servants the prophets"* (Amos 3:7).

Peter explains the mystery that God revealed to the prophets:

> *Of this salvation the prophets have inquired and searched carefully, who prophesied of the grace that would come to you, searching what, or what manner of time, the Spirit of Christ [Messiah] who was in them was indicating when He testified beforehand the suffering of Christ [Messiah] and the glories that would follow. To them it was revealed that, not to themselves, but to us they were ministering the things which now have been reported to you through those who have preached the gospel to you by the Holy Spirit sent from heaven—things which angels desire to look into (1 Peter 1:10-12).*

God's mystery is the eternal covenant that He made with Himself by which He would bring salvation to mankind. He would reconcile Jews and Gentiles to Himself and to each other through the blood of an everlasting covenant which He would make with Himself on our behalf. He would put His own Spirit within us so that we could share in His very own divine nature and live forever with Him in eternity. (See First Peter 1:3-4; Second Peter 1:1-4.)

The writer of Hebrews explains:

> *Now may the God of peace who brought up our Lord Jesus from the dead, that great Shepherd of the sheep, through the blood of the everlasting covenant, make you complete in every good work to do His will, working in you what is well pleasing in His sight, through Jesus Christ* [Messiah], *to whom be glory forever and ever. Amen* (Hebrews 13:20-21).

The prophets in the Hebrew Bible predicted it but did not fully understand everything they were prophesying. This is because its fulfillment would come later when God prepared for Himself a body and became one of us in the person of Jesus of Nazareth.

Peter further explains:

> *He* [Messiah] *indeed was foreordained before the foundation of the world, but was manifest in these last times for you who through Him believe in God, who raised Him from the dead and gave Him glory, so that your faith and hope are in God* (1 Peter 1:20-21).

Peter adds:

> *And so we have the prophetic word confirmed, which you do well to heed as a light that shines in a dark place, until the day dawns and the morning star rises in your hearts;*

knowing this first, that no prophecy of Scripture is of any private interpretation, for prophecy never came by the will of man, but holy men of God spoke as they were moved by the Holy Spirit (2 Peter 1:19-21).

God continues to reveal more of this divine mystery to His prophets, including John, who recorded it in the Book of Revelation. And not only did He reveal the mystery to His prophets, but to all of God's people who revere Him. King David explains, *"The secret of the LORD is with those who fear Him, and He will show them His covenant"* (Ps. 25:14).

We cannot see this mystery of God and this great end-time spiritual battle taking place with our physical eyes. It is all happening in the heaven or spiritual realm. We must have open spiritual eyes to see it. This is why the Lord gave John this vision. However, we can know that it is taking place by seeing the impact of it on the earth. What is happening in the heavens spiritually is manifested physically on the earth.

A good example of this is recorded in the Book of Second Kings. There we learn that the King of Syria sent his army at night to surround the city where the prophet Elisha was staying. The next morning, Elisha's servant went outside and saw the Syrian army surrounding the city. In a panic, he ran to Elisha and told him the situation. Elisha told his servant not to worry because they had more fighting for them than did the King of Syria. Of course the servant was completely confused by this answer. It was only he and Elisha.

Then Elisha asked God to open his servant's spiritual eyes so he could see the angelic army ready to fight on behalf of Elisha:

And Elisha prayed, and said, "LORD, I pray, open his eyes that he may see." Then the LORD opened the eyes of the young man, and he saw. And behold, the mountain was full of horses and chariots of fire all around Elisha (2 Kings 6:17).

So it is in the Book of Revelation. While we might not be able to see it with our physical eyes, God has a mighty army of angels fighting on our behalf. Although many are martyred during this time, they overcome death and stand in the presence of God, crying out for justice. The final answer to their prayers will be soon manifested in the blowing of the seventh trumpet-shofar judgment.

Eating God's Word (verses 8-11)

The same voice that told John to seal the words in the little book, now tells John to take the little book from the mighty angel and eat it. I don't know about you, but I would really be frightened to ask the angel to give me the book, much less reach out my hand to such a powerful being. It is good to be reminded that John is not literally doing this. He sees himself doing this in his apocalyptic vision. He is physically on the Isle of Patmos while spiritually, he is having this vision.

The mighty angel gives John the book, tells John to eat the book, and warns him that, although the words will be sweet in his mouth, they will turn bitter in his stomach. Sure enough, this is what John experiences. The words in the little book are sweet to the taste but upset his stomach. Now what is this about? Is John literally eating a book? I think we know the answer. John doesn't literally eat the book; he internalizes the words so that they become part of him.

We discover this same idea of eating God's words in the Hebrew Bible. The prophet Jeremiah used the same phrases, saying:

Your words were found, and I ate them, and Your word was to me the joy and rejoicing of my heart... (Jeremiah 15:16).

When the Lord spoke to Ezekiel, He told him to eat God's words. He meant that Ezekiel should spiritually digest God's Word so that it would become part of Ezekiel. The Lord said:

> *But you, son of man, hear what I say to you. Do not be rebellious like that rebellious house [Israel]; open your mouth and eat what I give you (Ezekiel 2:8).*

Ezekiel continued:

> *Now when I looked, there was a hand stretched out to me; and behold, a scroll of a book was in it. Then He spread it before me; and there was writing on the inside and on the outside, and written on it were lamentations and mourning and woe.*

> *Moreover He said to me, "Son of man, eat what you find; eat this scroll, and go, speak to the house of Israel." So I opened my mouth, and He caused me to eat that scroll. And He said to me, "Son of man, feed your belly, and fill your stomach with this scroll that I give you." So I ate, and it was in my mouth like honey in sweetness (Ezekiel 2:9-3:3).*

King David likened the Word of God to honey, saying it is *"More to be desired...than gold, yea, than much fine gold; sweeter also than honey and the honeycomb"* (Ps. 19:10).

Psalm 119 is the great chapter that explains the many benefits of the Word of God. In this psalm, we read: *"How sweet are Your words to my taste, sweeter than honey to my mouth!"* (Ps. 119:103).

There was a Jewish tradition to use honey on the first day of school for children just beginning their studies. The teacher would give the children an object containing the words of God coated with honey. The children were then instructed to lick the honey off the object, thus associating God's Word with the sweetness of the honey.

We are to digest God's Word so that it becomes part of us. God's Word should become bone of our bones and flesh of our flesh. God's Word should be alive in us with His very own life and power working in us, through us, and out of us.

God's Word is sweet to the soul. It is the real "comfort food" or "soul food." It gives us love when we feel unloved, peace when we are troubled, joy when we are depressed, hope when we are hopeless, faith when we are doubting, rest when we are stressed, and comfort when we are burdened.

Jesus Himself said, *"...Man shall not live by bread alone, but by every word that proceeds from the mouth of God"* (Matt. 4:4). The living Word of the living God has the capacity to impart God's own life into us. This is because God's spoken Word has His life in it. Just as when we speak, and our life or breath comes out of us to form our spoken words, when God speaks, the breath of His life comes out to form His words. When the Holy Spirit imparts those words to us, God's life comes into us through them.

Yet, God's Word can also be bitter when we have to speak His Word of judgment or correction to others or when He speaks it to us. That is not pleasant. God's Word of rebuke can cause us great grief and give us a spiritual stomach ache, so much so that we actually lose our physical appetite. We can become so anguished and heartsick about sin and its consequences, or about the fact that the wicked seem to prosper, or about the immorality all around us, that a time of prayer and fasting is the only thing that can console us.

This is what is happening to John. He is glad to receive the Word of God. It is sweet to the taste; but it gives him spiritual heartburn when he digests it. The words he will have to prophesy are unpleasant; they are words of more suffering and judgment.

The angel tells John that he will have to speak more prophecy. His audience will be the whole world, or as the Bible states it, *"many peoples, nations, tongues, and kings* [emperors]." The rest of the Book of Revelation contains the further prophecies John is to speak. Much of what John prophesies is bitter because it is about the further judgments of God on an anti-God world. However, the end of the prophecies is sweet, as they tell about the coming of the Lord to establish His Kingdom on the earth.

As today's believers, we have the prophetic words of John available to us. It is our responsibility to speak these words to our generation, as God commissioned Ezekiel to do. God put His words in Ezekiel and called him to be a watchman:

> *Son of man, I have made you a watchman for the house of Israel; therefore hear a word from My mouth, and give them warning from Me: when I say to the wicked; "You shall surely die" and you give him no warning, nor speak to warn the wicked from his wicked way, to save his life, that same wicked man shall die in his iniquity; but his blood I will require at your hand. Yet, if you warn the wicked, and he does not turn from his wickedness, nor from his wicked way, he shall die in his iniquity; but you have delivered your soul* (Ezekiel 3:17-19).

As watchmen, believers are to contemplate God, His plan of redemption, His counsel and decrees, and His prophetic season and words. We are to listen to what God is saying and we are to say it. We are to watch what God is doing and do it. We are to partner with God to observe, guard, protect, warn, and proclaim who He is in His nature and what He is doing in our world today. We must be alert to the prophetic season in which we are living. We must be single-minded, spiritually sober, and focused on the things of God. We must avoid being foolishly caught up in the things and cares of the world. We must be faithful and vigilant, particularly as we approach the "Day of the Lord."

REVIEW QUESTIONS

1. Write a summary of what you have learned in this lesson. Write the summary in clear, concise words as if you were going to present it to another person.

2. Write an explanation of how you can apply what you have learned in this lesson to your life.

3. Share what you have learned with your family, friends, and members of your study group.

ENDNOTE

1. Biblesoft's New Exhaustive Strong's Numbers and Concordance with Expanded Greek-Hebrew Dictionary. CD-ROM. Biblesoft, Inc. and International Bible Translators, Inc. (1994, 2003, 2006) s.v. "ischuros," (N.T. 2478).

Chapter 10

The Two Witnesses

REVELATION REVIEW

PERHAPS John thought he had seen enough when he learned that he had more prophecies to reveal about future events. A powerful angel appeared to John with a little book that contained the additional prophecies. John was told to take the book out of the angel's hand and eat the words. When he digested these prophecies, they were sweet in his mouth but turned sour in his stomach. They were sweet in that the prophecies revealed the ultimate victory of the Lord and His people over evil. Yet, when John fully realized that there was more suffering to come, the prophecies caused him much sorrow.

John heard seven voices so powerful that he compared them to thunder. As he was about to write the words of these seven thunderous voices, another voice from Heaven told him not to write what he heard yet. First the Lord desired to give John more detailed information about future events.

John recorded this additional information in chapters 10-15. This information does not seem to advance the chronology of the events but helps us know more about what is actually happening. Then in chapter

16, we learn that the seven thunderous voices were proclaiming the seven bowl judgments. This is the third of the three woes mentioned in Revelation 8:13. As previously stated, the story of the Book of Revelation actually ends with the last verses of chapter 11. In the rest of the Revelation, John is simply giving more details about the events.

In chapter 11, John is going to be introduced to two powerful witnesses of the Lord. They have an incredible ministry of prophecy and signs and wonders. Their prophecies are followed by miracles and demonstrate the Kingdom of God and the truth of their message. The witnesses are a great frustration to those who oppose God. The haters of God are even more irritated because the Lord supernaturally protects the two witnesses until their time of ministry is over. John tells us about the two witnesses. But before he does, he is told to measure the Temple of God. Let's join him now as he receives more revelation for our understanding.

THE TWO WITNESSES
(REVELATION 11:1-14)

Measuring the Temple of God (verses 1-2)

John is going to be an actual participant in this part of his vision. The angel gives John a measuring rod and tells him to measure the Temple, the altar, and the worshipers at the Temple. However, he tells John not to measure the outer court because that is the Court of the Gentiles. The angel further informs John that the Gentiles will attack the holy city of Jerusalem for 42 months or three and one-half years. This is apparently the last three and one-half years of the tribulation period. It is known as the Great Tribulation, a period of time Jesus mentioned in Matthew 24:21. This time period is also referred to by the phrase, *"time, times and half a time"* (Dan. 12:7; see Rev. 12:14.) In addition to the number of months and years, John also refers to this time in terms of 1,260 days (see Rev. 11:3; 12:6.)

Not all Christian theologians and scholars agree that the Jews will rebuild the Temple. They rightly understand that, as believers, our body is the temple of God; therefore, they question the need to build a literal Temple in Jerusalem. In their minds, God did away with the Jewish rituals when He allowed the destruction of the Temple. These are usually leaders of Christian denominations that teach replacement theology— the teaching that the Church replaced the Jews in God's covenantal plans. However, if this is true it means that God's covenant words cannot be trusted or that He is impotent to keep them.

Jewish theologians and scholars are also divided on this subject. While they do believe God will rebuild the Temple, some extreme Orthodox believe that only Messiah can do this and that it is blasphemous for Jews to attempt this without the Messiah. Others believe the Hebrew Scriptures say the Jews should rebuild the Temple in preparation for the coming of Messiah.

So does the Bible talk about a third Temple? The answer is clearly "yes." A very familiar Scripture is Isaiah 2:2-3 which says:

> *Now it shall come to pass in the latter days that the mountain of the LORD's house shall be established on the top of the mountains, and shall be exalted above the hills; and all nations shall flow to it. Many people shall come and say, "Come, and let us go up to the mountain of the LORD, to the house of the God of Jacob; He will teach us His ways, and we shall walk in His paths." For out of Zion shall go forth the law, and the word of the LORD from Jerusalem.*

In Daniel 9:27, the prophet talks about an evil person who will commit the *"abomination of desolation"* (Dan. 11:31). This refers to the stopping of sacrifices at the Temple. Some interpret this to be referring to Antiochus Epiphanes who desecrated the Temple by offering the blood of pigs on the holy altar of God during the time of the Maccabees. Others see this Scripture referring to the Romans when Titus destroyed the Temple in A.D. 70. Others believe Daniel is referring to a third Temple built at the end times.

In Matthew 24:15, Jesus referred to Daniel's prophecy and warned the believers to flee Jerusalem when they saw the Abomination of Desolation standing in the holy place. Again, some believe Jesus is referring to Titus rather than an end-time Temple. However, neither of these references could be speaking about Titus because he didn't enter the Temple. He burned it down.

In Second Thessalonians 2:1-4, Paul also refers to the Abomination of Desolation and says that he is the one *"who opposes and exalts himself above all that is called God or that is worshiped, so that he sits as God in the temple of God, showing himself that he is God"* (2 Thess. 2:4). Titus did not do this.

We noted at the beginning of this study that John most likely wrote the Book of Revelation in the late 90s of the first century. This was over 20 years after Titus burned down the Temple. If our dating is correct, John could not have been talking about that Temple.

In Revelation 11:1-2, John talks about the Temple of God and clearly puts it in the time of the Great Tribulation at the end of the age prior to the coming of Messiah. When we put all the Scriptures together, it is clear there will be a third Temple built before the coming of Messiah. It is a prophetic sign of the end times.

Why would God want to rebuild a Temple in Jerusalem? As non-Jewish believers, we know that when Jesus said, *"It is finished!"* (John 19:30), He meant that He was the once-and–for-all perfect sacrifice for sin. We know that, but Jewish people don't. And this is a Jewish Temple.

As is true of the Christian Church, the Jewish people are in need of a great spiritual awakening and revival. The Temple will be a great catalyst for this spiritual renewal. It will be like a magnet drawing Jews back to Israel and back to their covenant God. The Temple and the sacrifices offered at the Temple will be an important visual aid for the Jewish people to understand the necessity of a blood covenant sacrifice for sin. From a Christian view, this could point the Jewish people to Jesus and His death as the ultimate sacrifice for their sins.

The idea of building a Temple at the end of days is not just a Christian understanding. The core prayer of Judaism for thousands of years is called *The Amidah.* In this prayer, the Jewish people connect the rebuilding of Jerusalem and the Temple with the coming of Messiah. The 14th blessing says: "And to Jerusalem, Your city, may You return in compassion, and may You rest within it, as You have spoken. May You speedily establish the throne of David within it. Blessed are You, Hashem, the Builder of Jerusalem."[1]

The seventeenth blessing says: "Be favorable, Hashem, our God, toward Your people Israel and their prayer and restore the service to the Holy of Holies of Your Temple. The fire-offering of Israel and their prayer accept with love and favor, and may the service of Your people Israel always be favorable to You. Blessed are You, Hashem, Who restores His presence to Zion."[2]

God is going to restore His presence to Zion, that is, Jerusalem. While most of our Jewish friends do not realize it, and many Christians are ignorant of who Jesus really is, the Jewish Messiah and the Christian Savior and Lord are the same person. He is the Jewish *Yeshua* who is returning to His people in the land of Israel. The rebuilding of the Temple will hasten this glorious event.

As we observe prophetic events, do we see any sign of this Temple being built? Absolutely, yes! Most any Christian group who goes to Israel today will visit the Temple Institute under the direction of Rabbi Chaim Richman. Rabbi Richman tells us that 80 percent of all the vessels needed for Temple use have been made.

Furthermore, thousands of young men are being trained in the *Yeshivas* (Jewish Seminaries) in Israel to serve as priests at the Temple when it is built. All of us who go to the Christian celebration of *Suc-cot* in Jerusalem see this for ourselves at the Western Wall celebration led by these priests in training. This celebration is attended by many thousands of Israelis as well as hundreds, and perhaps thousands, of Christians.

Why does the angel tell John to measure the Temple, the altar, and the worshipers? There are several instances in the Hebrew Bible when God told His prophets to measure the Temple and Jerusalem; the earlier instructions were similar to what John is told to do by the angel.

For example, an angel told Ezekiel to measure the Temple that most likely represents the Temple during the Messianic age, what is commonly called the Millennium (see Ezek. 40). Zechariah saw a man who is going to measure Jerusalem (see Zech. 2:1-2). In three other references, the Bible mentions stretching out a line for measuring, both in building and destroying (see 2 Kings 21:12-14; Isa. 34:11; Lam. 2:8).

By reading these passages in context, we learn that when God speaks about measuring something, He is marking off territory—whether for blessing or judgment, protection or destruction. We do this today when determining the size of a lot for building purposes, or when we plan to demolish a structure. We mark off the land or building so as to separate it from the adjoining area.

Since John is told to measure the Temple, the altar, and the worshipers, we would understand this to mean that God is marking off the Temple and the people for protection. In the Zechariah passage, God says that He will be a wall of fire around Jerusalem (see Zech. 2:5).

Because John is told not to measure, or mark off, the Court of the Gentiles, we would understand that God will allow this area to be devastated by the Gentiles when they attack Jerusalem for the 42 months. This could be the time that Daniel, Jesus, and Paul wrote about in Scriptures we referenced earlier.

To better understand this situation, it helps to know that the Holy Temple courtyard was divided into two different areas. In the outer Court of the Gentiles, both Jews and devout Gentiles could assemble. But in the inner Court of the Jews only Jews were allowed. In order to keep this separation, the Jews had built a 4.5 foot high wall called the *Soreg* which divided the Court of the Gentiles from the Court of the Jews. The Jews placed many signs on the wall in strategic places warning Gentiles in Greek and Latin not to proceed or they would be killed. Several of these "stone billboards" have actually been discovered by archaeologists.

There is a story in the Book of Acts relating to this. The Jews erroneously believed that Paul had brought Gentiles into the Temple beyond the Court of the Gentiles. As a result, they sought to kill Paul. Acts reads:

> *Now when the seven days were almost ended, the Jews from Asia, seeing him [Paul] in the temple, stirred up the whole crowd and laid hands on him, crying out, "Men of Israel, help! This is the man who teaches all men everywhere against the people, the law, and this place; and furthermore he also brought Greeks into the temple and has defiled this holy place." (For they had previously seen Trophimus the Ephesian with him in the city, whom they supposed that Paul had brought into the temple)* (Acts 21:27-29).

During the time of Jesus, greedy merchants had set up their shops and booths in the Court of the Gentiles turning it into a marketplace. They took over the area so that there was no room for the Gentiles to worship God. This was the situation that angered Jesus to the point of overturning their product tables.

John wrote:

> *Now the Passover of the Jews was at hand, and Jesus went up to Jerusalem. And He found in the temple those who*

sold oxen and sheep and doves, and the money changers doing business. When He had made a whip of cords, he drove them all out of the temple, with the sheep and the oxen, and poured out the changers' money and overturned the tables. And He said to those who sold doves, "Take these things away! Do not make My Father's house a house of merchandise!" (John 2:13-16; see also Matthew 21:12-13.)

Western theologians and ministers tell us that God did away with His holy laws when Jesus died for our sins. Of the many Scriptures they quote to support their belief, one is Paul's statement in Ephesians which says:

For He Himself [Jesus] *is our peace, who has made both one* [Jew and Gentile], *and has broken down the middle wall of separation...* (Ephesians 2:14).

By misunderstanding the historical setting and misreading the rest of Paul's statement, they tell us that the middle wall of separation that Jesus broke down is the law of God. Paul's statement has nothing to do with the law of God. He is talking about the *Soreg* which separated Jews and Gentiles. He is talking about a physical wall in the Temple courtyard.

Because the Jews had a covenant relationship with God and the Gentiles didn't, the Jews were the chosen ones and the Gentiles were the pagans. This is what caused the enmity between Jews and Gentiles. God's covenant and His laws were just an outward manifestation of the enmity. But because Jesus died for both Jews and Gentiles, His death has made a way for Jews and Gentiles to be reconciled to God and to one another. We both have access to God. There is no more wall of separation. Spiritually speaking, the wall of separation has been torn down. Gentiles can now enter into the holy presence of God through the sacrifice of Jesus for our sins. Or as Paul said, *"For through Him we both have access by one Spirit to the Father"* (Eph. 2:18). Hallelujah!

The Two Witnesses (verses 3-6)

In the midst of all of the fighting, the Lord raises up two witnesses who prophesy for 1,260 days, or three and one-half years, or 42 months. John does not give the names of the two witnesses. Because of the nature of their miracles, some believe they are Moses and Elijah. But since Moses died, it does not seem likely that he is one these two witnesses. The only two people we know of in the Bible who never died are Enoch (see Gen. 5:21-24) and Elijah (see 2 Kings 2:1,9-12). Since John does not give their names, it really does no good to speculate.

John does say that the two witnesses are the two olive trees and the two lampstands standing before the God of the earth. He is referring to a Scripture in Zechariah where we are told that Zechariah had a vision of a lampstand with two olive trees, one on the right and the other on the left of the lampstand. Zechariah didn't know what his vision meant so he asked:

> *Then I answered and said to him, "What are these two olive trees—at the right hand of the lampstand and at its left?"* (Zechariah 4:11)

The angel answered, *"These are the two anointed ones, who stand beside the Lord of the whole earth"* (Zech. 4:14).

For Zechariah, the two anointed ones were Zerubbabel and Joshua. Zerubbabel was the governor of Judah while Joshua was the high priest. Both were involved in the rebuilding of the Temple. They both became discouraged in their efforts, which is why the Lord raised up Zechariah to encourage them.

The olive trees supply the oil for the lampstand, and in the Bible, oil is a symbol of the Holy Spirit. This is why the angel made the following statement to Zechariah: *"This is the word of the LORD to Zerubbabel: 'Not by might nor by power, but by My Spirit,' says the LORD of hosts"* (Zech. 4:6). In other words, Zerubbabel and Joshua would successfully complete their task of rebuilding the Temple because God's Spirit would empower them. God would enable them to do what they could not do in their own strength.

The two witnesses John sees are like Zerubbabel and Joshua in that God will empower them to do miraculous signs and wonders. The miracles are a testimony to the living God who is judging the people for their sin of rejecting Him. John notes that they are wearing sackcloth which is a garment of sadness and mourning. Even though the haters of God and His people seek to kill the two witnesses, God protects them for the three and one-half years of their ministry.

The Two Witnesses Are Killed (Verses 7-10)

When their appointed time of ministry is over, God allows the Beast to kill them. John explains that the Beast is the one that ascends out of the bottomless pit. Who is this Beast? It is interesting that the word *beast, when referring to evil,* is mentioned 37 times in the Book of Revelation. There is the Beast From the Sea, the Beast From the Earth, and in this reference, the beast from the bottomless pit. In the Book of Revelation the bottomless pit is also referred to as the sea (see Rev. 11:7; 13:1; 17:8.) The Beast From the Sea seems to be a reference to the anti-Messiah while the Beast From the Earth seems to be a reference to the False Prophet.

We discussed previously that the fifth trumpet-shofar (see Rev. 9:1-12), released tormenting demons from the bottomless pit, which is also called the abyss. As noted earlier, this is the biblical name for the abode of demons. It seems that the Beast coming out of the bottomless pit is satan. With God's permission, satan stirs up his followers to kill the two witnesses.

John explains that this is happening in Jerusalem. It is sad to read that John compares the spiritual condition of Jerusalem to Sodom and Egypt. Sodom represents the worse in immorality while Egypt is the biblical symbol of idolatry. This is not only a battle for the city of Jerusalem but also for the heart and soul of Jerusalem.

God made many promises in the Bible that He would return to Jerusalem at which time Jerusalem would become the throne of God (see Jer. 3:17). The battle for Jerusalem is satan's last desperate effort to rule the city in place of God. If the ministry of the two witnesses is happening during the last three and one-half years of the Great Tribulation, they are killed only a few days before the coming of Jesus described in Revelation 19.

Bible-believing people have great respect for the dead. Because of their beliefs about the next world, it is important that they honor the dead by burying them as quickly as possible.

In Psalm 79, the writer laments that the dead were not given a proper burial. This was after the Babylonians had destroyed Jerusalem in 586 B.C. He describes a situation similar to the scene John sees in Jerusalem:

> *O God, the nations have come into Your inheritance; Your holy temple they have defiled; they have laid Jerusalem in heaps. The dead bodies of your servants they have given as food for the birds of the heavens, the flesh of your saints to the beasts of the earth. Their blood they have shed like water all around Jerusalem, and there was no one to bury them* (Psalm 79:1-3).

Because of their satanic hatred of the two witnesses, those who killed them refused to bury them. Instead they left their bodies on display for three and one-half days. This was the greatest show of hatred, insult, and humiliation to the dead. Those who opposed God and His servants celebrated the death of the two witnesses with a party and exchanging of gifts. This most likely was seen around the world via satellite.

It is not unusual for tyrants to express their rage against their enemies in this way. For example, Eli Cohen was the greatest spy in the history of Israel. His mission was to uncover and reveal Syria's plans to attack Israel. Remarkably, Eli Cohen was so successful; he became third in line to be president of Syria. When he was finally discovered, the Syrians hanged him on May 18, 1965 and left his body on display for six hours. Tens of thousands of Syrians cheered and celebrated his death. As a final act of hatred, the Syrian government refused to give Eli's body to his family in Israel[3] so they could say *Kaddish*, the Jewish prayer to God honoring the dead.[4]

The Two Witnesses Resurrected (verses 11-14)

The celebration of the death of the two witnesses does not last very long. At the end of the three and one-half days, God breathes His life into the dead bodies of the two witnesses and they are resurrected. Can you imagine the startled look of horror and disbelief on the faces of the people of the world? By killing the two witnesses, they think they have killed God. Yet, God shows the world that they cannot kill Him.

When the two witnesses are resurrected, the people of the world hear a loud voice from Heaven calling God's servants to ascend to Heaven. The whole world sees this take place.

Similar language is used to describe the ascension of Jesus to Heaven as recorded in the Book of Acts:

> *Now when He [Jesus] had spoken these things, while they watched, He was taken up, and a cloud received Him out of their sight. And while they looked steadfastly toward heaven as He went up, behold, two men [angels] stood by them in white apparel, who also said, "Men of Galilee, why do you stand gazing up into heaven? This same Jesus, who was taken up from you into heaven, will so come in like manner as you saw Him go into heaven"* (Acts 1:9-11).

The prophecy about Jesus returning is about to be fulfilled in the Book of Revelation. But first, God calls His two witnesses to Heaven before He sends further judgment on those who oppose Him. John tells us that a great earthquake destroys a tenth of Jerusalem, causing the deaths of 7,000 people. Those who remain alive clearly recognize the hand of God and give Him glory. This does not necessarily mean that they repent, but that they simply acknowledge the obvious: the God of Heaven is the One True God who is the supreme sovereign Lord of the universe.

This brings an end to the second of the three woes. John learns that the third woe is at hand. This is the sounding of the seventh trumpet-shofar judgment which is the pouring out of the final bowls of God's wrath on the earth. While the seventh angel announces the blowing of the seventh trumpet-shofar, the judgments themselves are not described until Revelation 16. The rest of chapter 11 and chapters 12 through 15 do not advance the story in time but provide more details for our information.

REVIEW QUESTIONS

1. Write a summary of what you have learned in this lesson. Write the summary in clear, concise words as if you were going to present it to another person.

2. Write an explanation of how you can apply what you have learned in this lesson to your life.

3. Share what you have learned with your family, friends, and members of your study group.

Endnotes

1. "Rebuilding Jerusalem—Blessing Fourteen of the Amidah," *Hebrew for Christians,* http://www.hebrew4christians.com/Prayers/ Daily_Prayers/Shemoneh_Esrei/Jerusalem/jerusalem.html (accessed May 13, 2011).

2. "Avodah—Blessing Seventeen of the Amidah," *Hebrew for Christians,* http://www.hebrew4christians.com/Prayers/Daily_ Prayers/Shemoneh_Esrei/Avodah/avodah.html (accessed May 13, 2011).

3. Doron Geller, "Eli Cohen," Jewish Virtual Library, http://www. jewishvirtuallibrary.org/jsource/biography/Eli_Cohen.html (accessed May 13, 2011) and "Eli Cohen," *EliCohen.org,* http://www. elicohen.org/ (accessed May 13, 2011).

4. "The Meaning of Kaddish," *Kaddish Jerusalem,* http:// kaddishjerusalem.com/kaddish-prayer/ (accessed May 13, 2011).

Chapter 11

Proclaiming the Kingdom of God

REVELATION REVIEW

IN the blowing of the fourth trumpet-shofar judgment, the angel announced three woes that were yet to come. The first woe was the fifth trumpet-shofar judgment which was the releasing of demonic spirits from the bottomless pit. They were given authority by God for five months to torment only those who opposed God. God's people were protected from their attacks.

The second woe was the sixth trumpet-shofar judgment. God released the four angels or demonic spirits that had been bound at the Euphrates. They were given authority to send forth a 200-million-strong army to kill a third of mankind by fire, smoke, and brimstone. Whether John was describing an army of demonic spirits or a literal army with modern weapons, or both, releasing them brought further suffering to the unrighteous. Yet, they still refused to repent and turn to God.

In one last show of His call to repentance, God anointed the ministry of the two witnesses in Jerusalem for three and one-half years. The astounding miracles that God performed through them, clearly demonstrate that He is the supreme sovereign God of the universe. But instead of repenting, satan stirs up those who took his mark to kill the two witnesses. Thinking they have finally rid themselves of God's prophets, the world celebrated. But their victory party was premature. After their bodies were on display for three and-a-half days, God resurrected the two witnesses and took them to Heaven. He then sent an earthquake in Jerusalem as His response to the murder of his prophets.

PROCLAIMING THE KINGDOM OF GOD
(REVELATION 11:15-19)

Now it is time to announce the third woe which is the blowing of the seventh trumpet-shofar judgment. This is God's final judgment on unrepentant humankind before the coming of Jesus. The judgment is the proclamation that the Kingdom of God is now coming to the earth at which time God will destroy what is left of the kingdoms of the people of the world. This will be fulfilled in the return of Jesus described in Revelation 19. As previously noted, this last woe of the blowing of the seventh trumpet-shofar is described in Revelation 16. John is given more information about events that are taking place at this time, which is recorded in chapters 12 through 15.

The Kingdom of God (verse 15)

As just mentioned, the story in the Book of Revelation actually ends with the proclamation of the Kingdom of God in Revelation 11:15-19. The remaining chapters tell the same story, but give the details. A modern example would be the "instant replay" feature at sporting events. When a play is a completed, the referee makes his judgment about the play as he sees it. The opposing side (the enemy) may protest the referee's decision and call for an instant replay. When this happens, the referee looks at the play again through a viewer. He sees the same play but from different viewpoints and in more detail. After reviewing the instant replay, the referee's decision usually stands.

In a similar manner, when the angel proclaims the Kingdom of God, John sees the "end of the play." While God's enemies (satan and his followers) protest God's plans and purposes, John sees the end of the story with God judging the kingdoms of this world and establishing His Kingdom on the earth. In the rest of John's visions, He sees the "instant replay" of the same story, but in more detail. The decision of the referee (God) stands. The Lion of the Tribe of Judah has prevailed. He will rule over the nations from Mount Zion. Hallelujah!

Since the last trumpet-shofar judgment announces the Kingdom of God, I want to share some thoughts on His Kingdom. I believe clarification of this subject is critical to the times in which we are living. Most of the following material is taken from my book; *The End of All Things is at Hand: Are You Ready?*[1]

While the subject has not been emphasized by Christian ministers, the Kingdom of God is one of the most important subjects in the Bible. The clear consistent message from Genesis to Revelation is that God reigns over the earth. While God allows evil to have its way up to a point, He overrides evil and uses it to further His Kingdom purposes. The psalmist writes:

> *For the LORD most High is awesome; He is a Great King over all the earth....God reigns over the nations; God sits on His holy throne* (Psalm 47:2,8).

The Bible not only claims, but emphasizes, that God is the King and Lord to whom all nations and all people are accountable for the way they live. He is the Master of the universe and owner of all that He created. We do not own what God gives to us. We are only stewards and He will hold us accountable for how, when, where, and why we administer the resources He places in our hands.

American believers are greatly blessed to live in a democratic republic. But this blessing can also hinder our understanding of God as King. We have not lived under the rule of a monarch. Our founders left England because they did not want to live under the tyranny of bad kings. They put in place a Constitution so that we could live under the rule of law—not under the rule of a Sovereign King. So it is difficult for us to relate to God as King.

This is not only true for those of us who are Americans; it is also true for all of us as believers. We clearly see this evident in the way we present the Gospel. Our biblical presentation is not of God as King, but of God as Savior.

The Gospel of salvation is a wonderful Gospel. It has blessed the lives of millions of people and we honor those who faithfully proclaim it. But I want you to understand that our Gospel message is about to radically change. God is beginning to awaken His people to a greater awareness of the Gospel of the Kingdom. It is the Gospel of the Kingdom that is proclaimed in the Bible. As we draw nearer to the coming of the King, God is even now beginning to restore to us the principle, the proclamation, and the priority of the Gospel of the Kingdom.

WHAT IS THE KINGDOM OF GOD?

So what is the Gospel of the Kingdom? What do we mean when we talk about the Kingdom of God? It is most important that we understand that the Kingdom of God does not relate to time. This is very important. It is not a question of *when.* For example, the question of when Jesus will come and establish His Kingdom is not the issue. People erroneously want to relate the Kingdom of God to time. Therefore, they ask the question, "When?" The result of this thinking is to relegate the Kingdom of God to the future only. In the Bible, the Kingdom of God is not related to time. It is related to space. It is not a question of when, but where. What is the Kingdom of God and where is it?

The Kingdom of God is the rule of God over His creation. His Kingdom is everywhere present. It is expressed through the lives of His people who have chosen to live under His rule and who obey His royal decrees and commandments. By so doing, they manifest His Kingship on the earth. This is called "taking on the Yoke of the Kingdom." When Jesus said, *"Take My yoke upon you"* (Matt. 11:29), He meant we should acknowledge the Kingdom of God in our lives.

God has always had a people living under His rule. In this sense, the Kingdom of God is past, present, and future. But since God is outside of time, His Kingdom is always present. It always was, always is, and always will be. All people can experience God's Kingdom when they obey God's commandments and live under His rule.

Since Western Christians erroneously believe that grace means "no commandments," few experience Kingdom life. While all true believers live in God's Kingdom, they don't all experience God's Kingdom blessings because they don't keep His commandments.

God's commandments are His instructions for living in His Kingdom. His commandments are not the legalism of man-made rules. When Western preachers say that God "did away with the law," they give Christians the impression that being saved by grace means God places no demands on their lives. Nothing could be further from the truth. Yes, salvation is by grace alone but that grace empowers us to be liberated from ourselves; not from the rule of God.

Jesus said:

> *If you love Me, keep My commandments....He who has My commandments and keeps them, it is he who loves Me. And he who loves Me will be loved by My Father, and I will love him and manifest Myself to him* (John 14:15,21).

Can anything be clearer than this statement by Jesus?

GOD'S KINGDOM PAST

Adam and Eve

In the past, God's Kingdom rule was delegated to Adam who was given dominion over all of God's creation. He was only given one commandment, which he didn't keep. When Adam and Eve sinned, they no longer enjoyed God's Kingdom blessings. While God's Kingdom fills Heaven and Earth, we can only operate in it when we obey Him. With the exception of Noah, Adam and Eve's descendants chose not to live in God's Kingdom.

Abraham

Around 4,000 years ago, God created a new company of people through whom He would express His Kingdom to the world. Jewish tradition teaches that Abraham was the first person to address God as Master or Adonai (Lord), thus declaring His Kingdom over the world.

God declared that the descendants of Abraham, Isaac, and Jacob would be a unique people who would be a kingdom of priests to the nations. As they lived under His Kingship and obeyed His commandments, they would manifest His Kingdom to the nations (see Exod. 19:6).

At Sinai

At Sinai, God's chosen people said, *"All that the LORD has said we will do, and be obedient"* (Exod. 24:7). History teaches otherwise. As a company of people, the Jewish people have not lived up to their high calling. Even so, they do acknowledge God as King, even when they are not operating in His Kingdom.

Many believers have learned the first part of the Jewish blessing which says, *"Baruch ata Adonai, Eloheynu Melech Haolam,"* meaning,

"Blessed are You O Lord our God, King of the universe." God is King of the universe even though we may not personally acknowledge Him as King in our lives.

A central theme in Judaism is *Tikkun Olam* which in the Hebrew language means "repairing the world morally and spiritually." It is the vision of the prophets in the Bible to make the world a better place where justice and righteousness and peace—that is, Kingdom conditions—prevail over evil. We are not put on this earth as mere spectators to live a certain number of days on the earth and accumulate things. We are to actively partner with God in establishing His Kingdom on the earth, knowing that it will not fully come to Earth until Messiah comes to Earth as King and Lord of the nations.

King David

The Kingdom of God manifested on the earth is the focus and plan of the Bible. When God appointed David as king, David prayed to the Lord:

> *...Blessed are You, LORD God of Israel, our Father, forever and ever. Yours, O LORD is the greatness, the power and the glory, the victory and the majesty; for all that is in heaven and in earth is Yours; Yours is the kingdom, O LORD, and You are exalted as head over all* (1 Chronicles 29:10-11).

Psalms

The Kingdom of God was frequently acknowledged in the Book of Psalms. For example, Psalm 72:11 says, "*Yes, all kings shall fall down before Him; all nations shall serve Him.*"

Psalm 22:27-28 says:

> *All the ends of the world shall remember and turn to the LORD, and all the families of the nations shall worship*

before You. For the kingdom is the LORD's, and He rules over the nations.

The Prophets

The prophets also spoke about a golden age when God's Kingdom would be fully manifested on the earth. Daniel's words are an example:

> *And in the days of these kings the God of heaven will set up a kingdom which shall never be destroyed; and the kingdom shall not be left to other people; it shall break in pieces and consume all these kingdoms, and it shall stand forever* (Daniel 2:44).

Daniel 7:27 says:

> *Then the kingdom and dominion, and the greatness of the kingdoms under the whole heaven, shall be given to the people, the saints of the Most High. His kingdom is an everlasting kingdom, and all dominions shall serve and obey Him.*

Zechariah 14:9 says: *"The LORD shall be King over all the earth. In that day it shall be—the LORD is one, and His name one."*

Intertestamental Period

The Kingdom of God was also a major emphasis between Malachi and Matthew. Somewhere during that time, the Jewish people, out of reverence to God, were afraid they would misuse His name. A simple solution to their concern was simply not to say it. So instead of saying God's name, the Jews substituted other words which they considered to be synonyms for God's name.

For example, instead of saying the Kingdom of God, they would say the Kingdom of Heaven. Western scholars not connected to their biblical Hebraic roots have written volumes of pages and books trying to explain the difference between the Kingdom of God and the Kingdom of Heaven, not realizing that they are the same thing. This name substitution is similar to the respect shown by children to their parents; they don't call their parents by their first names, but by titles such as *Father* and *Mother* or *Dad* and *Mom*.

The following are examples of this practice:

> *It is easy for many to be hemmed in by few, for in the sight of Heaven, there is no difference between saving by many or by few. It is not on the size of the army that victory in battle depends, but strength comes from Heaven* (1 Maccabees 3:18-19 RSV).

> *And now let us cry to Heaven, to see whether He will favor us and remember His covenant with our ancestors and crush this army before us today* (1 Maccabees 4:10 RSV).

Clearly, God's people do not cry out to the place called Heaven, but to God Himself.

GOD'S KINGDOM PRESENT

John the Baptist and Jesus

While Christianity in America has not emphasized the Gospel of the Kingdom, it is the emphasis in the New Testament, which is a continuation of what was proclaimed in the Hebrew Bible. In between the writings of the two sections of the Bible, people often substituted the word *Heaven* for the name of God.

The Kingdom of God and the idea of grace and faith are not concepts that are new to the New Testament. All the writers of the New

Testament, with the possible exception of Luke, were Jews who received their concepts and understandings of the Kingdom of God and grace and faith from the writers of the Hebrew Bible beginning with the Book of Genesis. God's grace, and mercy operating through His kingdom is central to the teaching in the Hebrew Bible, what Christians call The Old Testament. The Kingdom of God is not only a past reality, it is a present reality extended to Gentiles who acknowledge Jesus as their King and live, by God's mercy and grace, under God's rule.

The New Testament opens with John the Baptist proclaiming, *"Repent, for the kingdom of heaven is at hand!"* (Matt. 3:2). Jesus had the same message in Matthew 4:17: *"Repent, for the kingdom of heaven is at hand."*

In Hebraic thinking, the phrase *at hand* means "imminent, bursting forth, ready to be revealed." Whenever Jesus did a miracle, it was a manifestation of the Kingdom of God in their midst. Jesus preached the Kingdom of God and then He demonstrated it by healing people and delivering them from demons.

Matthew 4:23 reads:

> *And Jesus went about all Galilee, teaching in their syna-gogues, preaching the gospel of the kingdom, and healing all kinds of sicknesses and all kinds of disease among the people.*

The most famous "Christian prayer" is really a Jewish prayer we have called the Lord's Prayer. In this prayer, Jesus prays to the Father, saying, "[May] *Your kingdom come.* [May] *Your will be done on earth as it is in heaven"* (Matt. 6:10). God's Kingdom is manifested on the earth when God's people do God's will.

In His greatest recorded teaching in the Bible, what we call the Sermon on the Mount, Jesus explained how to live as Kingdom people. And in Matthew 6:33, He essentially said to "seek first the Kingdom of

God and His righteousness and all these other things will be added to you."

After this teaching, Jesus sent His *talmidim* (disciples)[2] to preach the very same Gospel of the Kingdom. Matthew 10:7-8 reads:

> *And as you go, preach, saying, "The kingdom of heaven is at hand." Heal the sick, cleanse the lepers, raise the dead, cast out demons....*

Similarly, Luke 10:9 says, *"And heal the sick there, and say to them, 'The kingdom of God has come near to you.'"*

In a similar statement in Luke 17:21, Jesus said that the Kingdom of God is within your midst. The English translation says *"within you."*

In Matthew 8:11, Jesus said that the Gentiles will enter His Kingdom and become part of the Commonwealth of Israel.

In Matthew 24:14, Jesus said:

> *...This gospel of the kingdom will be preached in all the world as a witness to all the nations, and then the end will come.*

Paul and the Kingdom of God

Paul also focused his preaching on the Kingdom of God. Because we put so much emphasis on his message of faith and grace, we don't realize that this message was presented within the context of his central message of the Kingdom of God. Let's read Paul's own words as well as those of Luke, James, and Peter.

In Acts 14:22, Paul said, *"...We must through many tribulations enter the kingdom of God."* Acts 19:8 tells us: that "[Paul] *went into the synagogue and spoke boldly for three months, reasoning and persuading concerning the things of the kingdom of God."*

In Acts 20:25, Paul gave his farewell to the believers at Ephesus and reminded them that he preached to them the message of the Kingdom of God.

In Acts 28:23, when the Jews in Rome came to see Paul in prison, it says that Paul *"explained and solemnly testified of the kingdom of God, persuading them concerning Jesus from the Law of Moses and the Prophets, from morning till evening."*

In this story, we discover an incredible truth: the Gospel of Jesus is the Gospel of the Kingdom of God and this message is found in the Law of Moses and from the lips of the prophets.

Acts 28:30-31 reads:

> *Then Paul dwelt two whole years in his own rented house, and received all who came to him, preaching the kingdom of God and teaching the things which concern the Lord Jesus Christ* [Messiah] *with all confidence, no one forbidding him.*

In Acts 8:12, Phillip *"preached the things concerning the kingdom of God...."* In James 2:5 we are told that God has promised that those who love Him would be heirs of the Kingdom. Second Peter 1:11 tells us we can enter the everlasting Kingdom of our Lord.

GOD'S KINGDOM FUTURE

Finally, we learn in the Bible that God's Kingdom is not only past and present; it is also future, as the Scriptures declare.

In Matthew 25:34, Jesus said that those (the sheep) who give social assistance to His brethren (the Jews) will inherit God's Kingdom. It reads:

> *Then the King will say to those on His right hand, "Come, you blessed of My Father, inherit the kingdom prepared for you from the foundation of the world..."*

Revelation 11:15 is most interesting:

> *Then the seventh angel sounded: And there were loud voices in heaven, saying, "The kingdoms of this world have become the kingdoms of our Lord and of His Christ, and He shall reign forever and ever!"*

It seems that these loud voices are those of the angels of heaven proclaiming the final message of the Gospel of the Kingdom. Revelation 14:6 gives further clarification. This last trumpet-shofar judgment will bring the full measure of the Kingdom of God to Earth. As I have just shown, it has always been here in part, but with the King coming to Earth in person, the Kingdom of God will be fully manifested on Earth.

Revelation 20:1-6 tells us that God's covenant Kingdom people will reign with the Lord for 1,000 years on this earth.

Finally, we learn in Revelation 22:1-5 that God's Kingdom is everlasting, existing before the beginning of time and continuing after time is no more. The Lord God will reign into eternity over His creation as sovereign King and Master.

As we awaken to this shift of emphasis from the Gospel of Salvation to the Gospel of the Kingdom, from "Churchianity" to Kingdom life, we will soon see biblical kinds of miracles as being commonplace for ordinary believers who are willing to submit themselves to the Yoke of the Kingdom of God. The greatest outpouring of God's supernatural manifestations is at hand. While evil will increase, the glory of God's Spirit will anoint His people with His presence and His power as in the days of the first coming of Messiah. We see this happening in the ministry of the two witnesses.

We will soon see the time when the Kingdom of God in Heaven will so fill the earth, that God's people will be ready for the coming of the Lord. God's Kingdom is past, present, and future. It was, it is, and it is to come. May His Kingdom come, may His will be done on Earth as it is in Heaven (see Matt. 6:10). May we all embrace the Yoke of His Kingdom.

Kingdom Worship (verses 16-19)

When the elders hear the long awaited news that God is about to fully establish His Kingdom on the earth, they fall on their faces and worship God as *"the One who is and who was and who is to come"* (Rev. 11:17). He is the Almighty, the Great I AM who transcends time and space. His Kingdom that is forever will now be fully manifested in time on the earth in the person of the King Himself—Jesus of Nazareth, King of the Jews, and King of kings and Lord of lords. The great prayer that Jesus taught us to pray for God's Kingdom to come to Earth is being fully answered.

As world leaders realize that their rule without God is over, they are filled with anger and rage against Him. God is now going to pour out His final wrath against them which will forever destroy their godless "One World System." This transfer of kingdoms from the rule of man to the rule of God is the final fulfillment of Psalm 2.

The writer of that great psalm looked into the future and proclaimed:

> *Why do the nations rage, and the people plot a vain thing? The kings of the earth set themselves, and the rulers take counsel together, against the LORD and against His Anointed* [the Messiah], *saying, "Let us break Their bonds in pieces and cast away Their cords from us"* (Psalm 2:1-3).

These world leaders are so deceived as to think they can defeat God. The Lord's response is to laugh at their foolish arrogance:

> *He who sits in the heavens shall laugh; the Lord shall hold them in derision. Then He shall speak to them in His wrath, and distress them in His deep displeasure: "Yet, I*

have set My King [the Messiah] *on My holy hill of Zion* [Jerusalem]" (Psalm 2:4-6).

The psalmist then sees God proclaiming His Kingdom:

I will declare the decree: the LORD has said to Me [the Messiah], *"You are My Son, today I have begotten You* [have begun Your Kingdom rule on the earth]. *Ask of Me, and I will give you the nations for Your inheritance, and the ends of the earth for your possession. You shall break them with a rod of iron; You shall dash them to pieces like a potter's vessel"* (Psalm 2:7-9).

Writing with clear spiritual eyes, the psalmist sees God giving His final warning to world leaders:

Now therefore, be wise, O kings; be instructed, you judges of the earth. Serve the LORD with fear, and rejoice with trembling. Kiss the Son [bow down in humble submission], *lest He be angry, and you perish in the way, when His wrath is kindled but a little. Blessed are all those who put their trust in Him* (Psalm 2:10-12).

When Messiah comes to set up His Kingdom, the righteous dead will be raised and rewarded for their faithfulness to worship and serve the One True God through their faith and trust in His Son. They will rule and reign with Him as explained throughout the Scriptures. But the unrighteous will be judged and forever banished from the presence of God.

Looking forward to this time, an angel gave the following words of comfort and assurance to Daniel:

Many of those who sleep in the dust of the earth shall awake, some to everlasting life, some to shame and everlasting contempt (Daniel 12:2).

Jesus explained it this way:

> *Most assuredly, I say to you, he who hears My word and
> believes in Him who sent Me has everlasting life, and shall
> not come into judgment, but has passed from death into
> life. Most assuredly, I say to you, the hour is coming, and
> now is, when the dead will hear the voice of the Son of
> God; and those who hear will live. For as the Father has
> life in Himself, so He has granted the Son to have life in
> Himself, and has given Him authority to execute judgment
> also, because He is the Son of Man. Do not marvel at this;
> for the hour is coming in which all who are in the graves
> will hear His voice and come forth—those who have done
> good* [acceptable to God], *to the resurrection of life, and
> those who have done evil* [unacceptable to God], *to the
> resurrection of condemnation* (John 5:24-29).

Almost as a footnote to this proclamation and worship, John sees
the Ark of the Covenant in the Holy of Holies of the Temple in Heaven.
Bible students recall that when God delivered the Hebrews from Egypt,
He instructed them to build a tabernacle or tent where He would dwell
among them. God's glorious presence resided in the inner room—the
Holy of Holies above the Ark of the Covenant.

The Ark of the Covenant was a small chest with statues of cherubim
attached to the lid. This represented the throne of God on the earth at
that time. It was the way God chose to dwell among His people. Later,
David brought the Ark of the Covenant to the City of David and placed
it in the tent he built to worship the Lord. When Solomon built the
Temple, he had a great dedication service at which time he moved the
Ark from the City of David to the Temple. The glory of the Lord so filled
the Temple that the priests could no longer minister. All they could do
was worship God.

Second Chronicles reads:

> *And it came to pass when the priests came out of the Most Holy Place (for all the priests who were present had sanctified themselves, without keeping to their divisions), and the Levites who were the singers, all those of Asaph and Heman and Jeduthun, with their sons and their brethren, stood at the east end of the altar, clothed in white linen, having cymbals, stringed instruments and harps, and with them one hundred and twenty priests sounding with trumpets—indeed it came to pass, when the trumpeters and singers were as one, to make one sound to be heard in praising and thanking the LORD, and when they lifted up their voice with the trumpets and cymbals and instruments of music, and praised the LORD saying, "For He is good, for His mercy endures forever," that the house, the house of the LORD, was filled with a cloud, so that the priests could not continue ministering because of the cloud; for the glory of the LORD filled the house of God (2 Chronicles 5:11-14).*

The connection between the worship when Solomon dedicated the Temple to what John sees in Heaven should be obvious. When John says that he sees the Ark of the Covenant, his readers would understand that he was seeing the throne room and presence of God. Like the priests at the dedication of the Temple, the 24 elders (the representative number of all of God's people) fall down and worship God.

As He did with the opening of the seventh seal and the pouring out of the seventh bowl judgment, God endorses what John has written with lightnings, noises, thunderings, an earthquake, and great hail (see Rev. 8:5; 16:18-21). This is God's way of saying, "Amen!"

REVIEW QUESTIONS

1. Write a summary of what you have learned in this lesson. Write the summary in clear concise words as if you are going to present it to another person.

2. Write an explanation of how you can apply what you have learned in this lesson to your life.

3. Share what you have learned with your family, friends, and members of your study group.

ENDNOTES

1. Available at my online bookstore at www.rbooker.com.

2. Richard Amiel McGough, "Spoke 12—Lamed," *Bible Wheel,* http://www.biblewheel.com/wheel/spokes/Lamed_Disciples.asp (accessed May 14, 2011).

Chapter 12

War in Heaven and on Earth

REVELATION REVIEW

AS we continue with our study, it is good to be reminded that the Book of Revelation is written as apocalyptic literature. As explained previously, in this style of writing, the author claims to have spiritual visions or to have been spiritually transported into the heavens where he is made to understand divine mysteries that are hidden to us. He sees in Heaven spiritual realities that are invisible to us but are manifested visibly on the earth. Since we can only see the visible manifestations on the earth, we are not aware that the things happening in our world are like a mirror showing us the activities of Heaven. We need an apocalyptic visionary to explain them to us.

In trying to understand difficult times, we often ask ourselves and others, "What in the world is going on"? Or "What is this world coming to"? Apocalyptic literature answers these questions. The writer explains Heaven's mysteries using symbols we can understand. The symbols are not intended to be interpreted literally, but represent real people and real events that the readers would understand in their times.

We clearly see this in the following chapters where John sees a number of personalities that represent real people and events of his time as well as the end times. While those living in John's time would have understood the meaning of his symbols, we who live today are not so fortunate. Because the symbols John used represent people and events of 2,000 years ago, we have to interpret them in light of history and our own times. This is the challenge of modern scholars and students of the Bible.

War in Heaven and on Earth
(Revelation 12)

In Revelation chapters 12 and 13, John sees six personalities. These are: 1) a woman clothed with the sun, 2) a red dragon, 3) a male Child, 4) Michael, 5) the Beast From the Sea, and 6) the Beast From the Earth. Let's now continue to read what John saw and the symbols he used to explain these personalities. We will seek to understand these symbols both as John's readers would have understood them and as they apply in our times.

The Sign of the Woman (verses 1-2)

John informs us that he sees a great sign. The Greek word that John uses for sign is *semeion*. It refers to a supernatural signal or indication that something was about to happen on the earth.[1] Ancient people believed that signs in the heavens were messages to them that changes were coming to the earth. John uses apocalyptic language that people of his time would understand. This would be no ordinary sign, but a great sign meaning something extraordinary is going to happen.

The sign that he sees is a woman. She is clothed with the sun, has the moon under her feet, and wears a garland or crown of 12 stars. The woman is pregnant to the point of having labor pains and is about ready to give birth. Wow, that is some sign. What is this all about?

While scholars present different interpretations of the meaning of this sign, we must look to the Bible for our guidance. I believe the Book of Genesis provides the answer to its meaning; it is found in the story of Joseph.

You may recall that Joseph was the favorite son of Jacob (Israel). Joseph had a dream in which his brothers bowed down to him (see Gen. 37:5-8). Joseph was only 17 years of age when he had this dream, so he didn't have enough wisdom to keep it to himself. Naturally his brothers, who were older, resented Joseph for his arrogance.

Joseph had a second dream. In this dream, his brothers and parents bowed down to him. Genesis tells what happened next:

> *Then he dreamed still another dream and told it to his brothers, and said, "Look, I have dreamed another dream. And this time, the sun, the moon, and the eleven stars bowed down to me" (Genesis 37:9).*

When Joseph told his father and his brothers about the second dream, they scorned him even more. Yet, his father put the dream in the back of his mind and thought about it.

Joseph's dream was fulfilled years later in Egypt when Pharaoh made Joseph his second-in-command. When Joseph's brothers came to Egypt seeking food, they did not recognize Joseph, but bowed before him:

> *And when Joseph came home, they brought him the present which was in their hand into the house, and bowed down before him to the earth. Then he asked them about their well-being, and said, "Is your father well, the old man of whom you spoke? Is he still alive?" And they answered, "Your servant our father is in good health; he is still alive." And they bowed their heads down and prostrated themselves (Genesis 43:26-28).*

Considered in light of this story from Genesis, the woman whom John sees is Israel. John does a flashback to the Jewish patriarchs and the promise God gave them to be the bearers of the Redeemer of mankind. The sun represents Jacob, the moon represents Rachel, and the 12 stars represent the 12 children or tribes of Israel.

The descendants of Abraham, Isaac, and Jacob (Israel) were the covenant people through whom God would bring the Messiah into the world. The woman crying out in pain symbolizes Israel suffering for centuries at the hands of the Gentiles while waiting for the birth of their Deliverer, the Messiah, Jesus of Nazareth. This sign reminds us that God also gave a sign in the heavens recorded in the New Testament when the Messiah was born to Mary, a descendant of the tribe of Judah.

When Jesus was born, the Jews were suffering greatly under the cruel rule of the Romans. God sent them a sign in the heavens that something remarkable was about to happen. This sign was the star of Bethlehem which guided the wise men (astronomers) from the East to Jerusalem. When they saw the sign in Heaven, they connected it to a great event that was to happen on the earth, the birth of the King of the Jews. When they asked Herod exactly where the King of the Jews was born, he directed them to Bethlehem (see Matt. 2:1-8) according to the prophecy in Micah 5:2.

Out of fear, Herod killed all the baby boys two years old and under. Matthew said that this massacre fulfilled the prophecy of Jeremiah of Rachel weeping for her children. (See Matthew 2:1-18.) Jesus was born in these circumstances of intense Jewish suffering.

The Sign of the Red Dragon (verses 3-4)

The next sign John sees is a great, fiery red dragon. This frightening monster has seven heads, ten horns, and seven diadems or crowns on his head. In verse 9, we learn that the dragon symbolizes the devil or satan.

In apocalyptic language, the seven heads, ten horns, and seven crowns represent nations and world leaders over which satan will rule in the end times. Since the number seven often means completion, the idea is that satan will have complete power and authority over a world united under his control. Only God's people, and apparently some strong-willed independent holdouts, who refuse the Mark of the Beast, do not submit to him. This is why satan energizes his puppet world leaders to persecute God's people. John gives further information in Revelation 13 and Revelation 17 where he tells us about the Beast From the Sea and the Beast From the Earth.

The description connects to Daniel's prophecy about four great Gentile "beast" empires that will rule over Israel throughout history. Daniel wrote: *"Four great beasts came up from the sea, each different from the other"* (Dan. 7:3). In the next few verses, Daniel described these beast empires which most scholars understand to be Babylon, Persia, Greece, and Rome.

Daniel described the last empire with these words:

> *After this I saw in the night visions, and behold a fourth beast, dreadful and terrible, exceedingly strong. It had huge iron teeth; it was devouring, breaking in pieces, and trampling the residue with its feet. It was different from all the beasts that were before it, and it had ten horns* (Daniel 7:7).

In verse 24, Daniel explained that the ten horns are ten kings.

These beast empires are the same that Daniel saw when he interpreted King Nebuchadnezzar's dream as recorded in Daniel 2. The king saw a great image in his dream. This so troubled him that he asked Daniel to interpret the dream. Daniel explained the dream to the king. The head of gold represented Babylon; the chest and arms of silver represented Persia; the belly and thighs of bronze represented Greece; and the legs of iron represented Rome. The feet of iron and clay with the ten toes correspond to the ten horns of Revelation. Daniel then sees a great mountain (kingdom) that destroys the image. Daniel explains that the great mountain is the Kingdom of God coming to Earth. (See Daniel 2:31-45.)

In Daniel 2, these kingdoms of men are described in terms of precious metals. This is how mankind sees himself in his pride and arrogance. In Daniel 7, these kingdoms are described as beasts. This is how God sees the efforts of mankind to rule without Him.

The Book of Daniel, particularly chapters 2, 7, and 12, provide critical background information for understanding John's vision of the end-time "beast empire." Therefore, it is important to take time to carefully read these chapters while studying the remaining chapters in the Book of Revelation. It is also important that you do not get bogged down trying to figure out every detail of every symbol. It is more important to see the big picture and have an intimate relationship with the Lord. As these events unfold, God will show us how they play out on the stage of world history.

In Revelation 12:4 John reports that he saw satan's tail pulling one-third of the stars from Heaven to Earth. Once again, we remind ourselves that John is using symbolic language. He does not mean that satan literally has a tail or that a third of the physical stars in the sky follow satan. What he means is that he was able to see with spiritual eyes the spiritual battles taking place in the spirit world in Heaven. John tells us more about this in the next few verses when he describes a rebellion in Heaven.

John sees satan confronting the woman (Israel) when she is about to give birth to a child. Satan is waiting for the child to be born so he can kill the baby at birth. This is not just any child satan wants to destroy. John is talking about the birth of the Redeemer of mankind—the Messiah, Jesus of Nazareth. Israel is personified in the woman who is to give birth to the Messiah.

We know from the Bible that satan attempted to kill Jesus from the moment He was born. As just mentioned, when King Herod learned of the birth of the King of the Jews, he killed all the baby boys two years old and under. It was satan working through Herod in this demonically-inspired act. Although satan failed in this attempt, he did not give up in his relentless attacks against Jesus.

For example, Matthew tells us that satan advised Jesus to tempt God by jumping off the pinnacle of the Temple (see Matt. 4:5-6). This was before Jesus even began His ministry. Jesus would have died prematurely and failed to accomplish the purpose for which He was born. When Jesus gave His very first teaching in Nazareth, satan stirred up the crowd to throw Jesus off the cliff, but Jesus avoided them (see Luke 4:28-30). Finally, satan found a willing vessel in Judas who betrayed Jesus to the Romans (see Matt. 26:47-56). While Pilate had Jesus executed, Jesus made it clear that it was God who allowed Pilate to make this decision (see John 19:11).

The Male Child (verses 5-6)

John further comments that God caught up Jesus (the Child) to His throne in Heaven. As the Lamb of God, Jesus bore the sins of mankind for us. He was the innocent once-and-for-all substitutionary sacrifice for sin. Isaiah prophesied this defining moment in history:

> *Surely He has borne our griefs and carried our sorrows; yet we esteemed Him stricken, smitten by God, and afflicted. But He was wounded for our transgressions, He was bruised for our iniquities; the chastisement for our peace was upon Him, and by His stripes we are healed. All we like sheep have gone astray; we have turned, every one, to his own way; and the Lord has laid on Him the iniquity of us all* (Isaiah 53:4-6).

Because Jesus had never sinned, He knew the prophecy in the Book of Psalms stating that God would not allow His soul to stay in the place of the dead or His body to be corrupted:

> *Therefore my heart is glad, and my glory* [my soul][2] *rejoices; my flesh also will rest in hope. For You will not leave my soul in Sheol, nor will You allow Your Holy One to see corruption* (Psalm 16:9-10).

Acts records the ascension or "catching up" of Jesus to Heaven:

> *Now when He had spoken these things, while they watched, He was taken up, and a cloud received Him out of their sight. And while they looked steadfastly toward heaven as He went up, behold, two men* [angels] *stood by them in white apparel, who also said, "Men of Galilee, why do you stand gazing up into heaven? This same Jesus, who was taken up from you into heaven, will so come in like manner as you saw Him go into heaven"* (Acts 1:9-11).

John further identifies this male Child by referring to the Psalm 2 prophecies we have already explained. Because Jesus is returning as the Lion of the Tribe of Judah, He will rule over Israel as the King of the Jews and over the nations as King of kings and Lord of lords. As God in human flesh, Jesus will rule with absolute authority and power, or as John says, *"with a rod of iron"* (Rev. 19:15).

Now that satan can no longer attack Jesus, he turns his hatred against the woman; that is Israel and the non-Jewish followers of Jesus. John gives more details in the rest of this chapter. For now he just says that God's people flee to a place of safety where God takes care of them for 1,260 days, or three and one-half years. This is apparently the same time period in which the two witnesses are ministering, which seems to be the last half of the tribulation, known as the Great Tribulation.

Michael the Archangel (verses 7-12)

The fourth personality John sees is Michael, along with his angels. Michael is mentioned five times in the Bible (see Dan. 10:13,21; 12:1; Jude 9; Rev. 12:7). I commented previously that Michael is one of the archangels of God. He is also the guardian angel of Israel (see Dan. 10:21; 12:1).

In these verses, John pauses in his writing about the dragon attacking the woman. He will resume the story at the end of the chapter. The reason he pauses is to explain to us the spiritual warfare and rebellion he sees in Heaven. This is the event Daniel saw as recorded in Daniel 12. It is the beginning of the Great Tribulation.

Daniel writes:

> *At that time Michael shall stand up, the great prince who stands watch over the sons of your people; and there shall be a time of trouble, such as never was since there was a nation, even to that time. And at that time your people shall be delivered, everyone who is found written in the book* (Daniel 12:1).

John tells us that Michael and his angels fight a war against the dragon and his angels. John identifies the dragon as the devil and satan. The word *devil* means "slanderer" or "false accuser"[3] while *satan* means "adversary."[4]

Many people doubt the reality of a literal, personal devil. They believe the devil is just a character out of the imagination of man's mind. They think of him as a strange character in a red suit with a long tail, horns, and a pitchfork. This image came about in the Middle Ages when the devil was portrayed this way in plays so the audience could recognize his character when he came onto the stage.

Nothing could be further from the truth about what the devil is really like. There really is a personal devil and a spirit world that we cannot comprehend with our physical senses. Whether one believes this or not, does not change its reality.

There are two passages in the Hebrew Bible that many scholars believe refer to satan's origin and fall. These are Isaiah 14:10-15 and Ezekiel 28:12-19. In their immediate historical context, the Isaiah Scripture literally refers to the rise and fall of the king of Babylon while the Ezekiel Scripture refers to the king of Tyre in the same way. With this in mind, the wording in these verses seems to go far beyond addressing mere human kings; instead it uses them as examples to aid us in understanding the fall of satan.

Briefly, the Bible would have us understand that satan was at one time called lucifer. This name means "light-bearer."[5] Lucifer was God's most perfect, splendid creation. It seems that he was the top-ranking angel and served at God's throne. His outward appearance was iridescent, like a magnificent rainbow reflecting the glory of God.

When God created lucifer, He created him perfect in every way. People often ask "How could a good God create an evil being like the devil?" Because there is such a contradiction of a good God creating an evil being, they conclude there must not really be a devil. Part of this reasoning is correct. God did not create lucifer as an evil being. He created lucifer as the most glorious of all of His angelic beings for the purpose of serving Him and reflecting His glory. Some scholars believe that lucifer was actually God's heavenly praise and worship leader.

However, because of the sin of pride, lucifer desired the worship for himself. He led a rebellion in Heaven against God. According to John's words, lucifer convinced a third of the stars (angels) to follow him (see Rev. 12:4,7,9; 2 Pet. 2:4; Jude 6). It was lucifer who introduced sin and evil into God's world.

Jesus saw this in the Spirit and said to His disciples, *"I saw Satan fall like lightning from heaven"* (Luke 10:18).

Of course, God could not allow this rebellion. While giving lucifer limited access to His presence, God stripped him of his glorious position. Lucifer then became known as satan or the devil. The angels that followed him became his demonic army. As I have shared previously, some of these demons are so powerful that God assigned them to the bottomless pit until the end times when He releases them as judgment against those who oppose Him. He allows the other demons limited freedom to serve satan and attack human beings in what believers call *spiritual warfare.*

While satan lost in his attempt to be worshiped in Heaven, he did not give up. His pride and hatred of God drove him to establish his worship and rule on the earth. He has done this by creating a world system that is anti-God. This satan desires to live out his god-image by ruling over this world system. This will find its climax as described in the following chapters in the Book of Revelation.

Working behind the scenes through his human servants, the anti-Messiah and False Prophet, satan will establish the final form of his one-world political-religious-economic-military-social system. We call it "the New World Order." Nonbelievers will unwittingly worship satan by taking the Mark of the Beast.

With his limited access to God, satan constantly slanders and accuses God's people of being unworthy of God's grace and mercy. It is as if satan is taunting God to cast away the believers with the same judgment God gave him.

For example, we learn in the Book of Job that satan came before God and accused Job of worshiping and serving God only to get God's blessings (see Job 1:6-12). The Lord knew Job's heart and gave satan permission to test Job. Bible students know that Job suffered greatly but stayed true to God. God was honored, Job was vindicated, and satan proved himself to be a liar who falsely accused Job.

On another occasion, we learn in Zechariah that satan accused Joshua the high priest of serving God in stained garments. In other words, Joshua was not holy enough to be the high priest. The Lord rebuked satan, forgave Joshua of any sin, and clothed him in clean garments. (See Zechariah 3:1-5.)

Apparently, satan still has this limited access to God. He is still the *"accuser of our brethren"* (Rev. 12:10). But believers have a High Priest who lives forever to make intercession for us (see Heb. 7:25). When satan accuses us before God and when we feel conviction of sin, we can find forgiveness and be made spiritually clean through the blood of Jesus. When we accept the blood of the everlasting covenant for ourselves, God forgives our sins to be remembered no more. He casts them into the sea of forgetfulness. He separates us from our sins as far as the east is from the west. (See Hebrews 7-9.) Thank You, Lord.

We learn from John that God finally banishes satan from His presence. The devil is cast out of Heaven; since he no longer has access to God to slander His people, he now vents his wrath against people alive on the earth during this time. He deceives the nonbelievers to embrace the "New World Order" of peace and unity while persecuting God's people who refuse to take his mark. Because they are deceived by satan, those who take his mark will now accuse the believers of being obstacles to world peace and enemies of the State.

While John is seeing all of this, he hears a loud voice proclaiming the Lord's final victory and judgment of satan. The fullness of the Kingdom of God is about to be revealed. Jesus will soon return. The righteous will prevail and rule with the Lord on the earth. Believers in Heaven and believers on the earth rejoice. Even though they are persecuted and martyred, God's people overcome satan through the blood of the Lamb and the word of their testimony (see Rev. 12:11). But those who oppose God also face the fierce wrath of satan, because he knows he only has a short time (three and one-half years) to deceive them into worshiping him.

Those who take the Mark of the Beast think that this will help them overcome their struggles to survive and prosper. But it is a tragic deception. The real overcomers are those who are willing to die for their faith. As Jesus said:

> *Most assuredly, I say to you, unless a grain of wheat falls into the ground and dies, it remains alone; but if it dies, it produces much grain* [fruit]. *He who loves his life will lose it, and he who hates* [does not prefer] *his life in this world will keep it for eternal life* (John 12:24-25).

Satan Persecutes the Woman (verses 13-17)

John now resumes his comments from verse 6 about the dragon (satan) attacking the woman. As noted, the woman represents Israel. John explains that the Lord supernaturally protects and cares for (nourishes) Israel during this three and one-half year period. This situation is similar to when God provided manna in the desert for the children of Israel (see Exod. 16:4) and nourishment for Elijah when he was in the desert (see 1 Kings 17:2-4). God is still able to supernaturally take care of His people and He will do so during the Great Tribulation. As King David said:

> *I have been young, and now am old; yet I have not seen the righteous forsaken, nor his descendants begging bread* (Psalm 37:25).

Using apocalyptic symbolism, John says that the woman was given two wings of a great eagle so she could fly into the wilderness (desert) in safety. The Lord has used this wording before as a figure of speech. When the Lord delivered the Hebrews from Egypt, He brought them into the desert and cared for them for 40 years. Exodus reads: "*You have seen what I did to the Egyptians, and how I bore you on eagles' wings and brought you to Myself*" (Exod. 19:4). Similar wording is found in Deuteronomy 32:11-12. Obviously, the eagles' wings do not signify the United States providing some kind of airlift to save the Jews.

Jesus warned His disciples that Jerusalem would be attacked. This happened in the first Jewish revolt against the Romans. The war lasted for seven years from A.D. 66-73. Titus invaded Jerusalem and burned the city and the Temple in A.D. 70. Jesus had already told His disciples to flee to the mountains. Historians tell us that when the war began, the disciples fled east of the Jordan River to the desert town of Pella where God protected them from being completed annihilated by the Romans.

Some scholars believe that this was the complete fulfillment of Jesus' prophecy. However, in spite of legends to the contrary, Titus did not go into the Holy of Holies in the Temple. While there are clear parallels, Jesus' words are in the context of the period of the Great Tribulation which John is now describing (see Matt. 24:15-28). This is similar to what happened when the Romans attacked Jerusalem, except this time, the situation is so bad the Lord will have to intervene through the coming of Jesus.

Jesus explains:

> For then there will be great tribulation, such as has not been since the beginning of the world until this time, no, nor ever shall be. And unless those days were shortened, no flesh would be saved; but for the elect's sake those days will be shortened (Matthew 24:21-22).

The devil, or satan, also referred to as "the serpent" (see Gen. 3:1-15), seeks to drown the woman, but the Lord sends an earthquake to divert the water. Whether this is symbolic or meant to be taken literally, we don't know. The Bible often uses flood terminology as a symbol of great evil and distress. Isaiah described such times: "...*When the enemy comes in like a flood, the Spirit of the LORD will lift up a standard against him*" (Isa. 59:19). In this instance, the water could be symbolic of satan's army pursuing the woman. We will know when we see it happening.

There are also numerous examples in the Hebrew Bible of God using the natural elements to destroy His enemies and the enemies of

His people. God literally drowned Pharaoh's army when they were pursuing the children of Israel. Whatever the exact interpretation of these verses, the point is that they show satan doing everything he can to kill God's people. Yet, God hinders him with both natural and supernatural means.

When satan realizes that he can't destroy Israel, he redirects his efforts against the rest of God's people. In verse 17, John refers to these believers as the *"rest of her offspring, who keep the commandments of God and have the testimony of Jesus Christ* [Messiah]*."*

Whether you believe these are the grafted-in Gentiles who are part of the Commonwealth of Israel or those newly saved during the Great Tribulation is a matter of interpretation. What we do know for sure is that they are believers who keep the commandments of God. This certainly refutes Western Christian teaching that salvation by grace through faith means that believers are free from the commandments of God. There will be no casual, cultural, carnal, worldly, half-committed believers at this time.

As Jesus said:

> *He who has My commandments and keeps them, it is he who loves Me. And he who loves Me will be loved by My Father, and I will love him and manifest Myself to him* (John 14:21).

With this background, John next introduces us to satan's two most important disciples, the Beast From the Sea and the Beast From the Earth. Let's join him in Volume 3 of this series as he shares this part of his vision.

REVIEW QUESTIONS

1. Write a summary of what you have learned in this lesson. Write the summary in clear, concise words as if you were going to present it to another person.

2. Write an explanation of how you can apply what you have learned in this lesson to your life.

3. Share what you have learned with your family, friends, and members of your study group.

ENDNOTES

1. Biblesoft's New Exhaustive Strong's Numbers and Concordance with Expanded Greek-Hebrew Dictionary. CD-ROM. Biblesoft, Inc. and International Bible Translators, Inc. (1994, 2003, 2006) s.v. "semeion," (N.T. 4592).

2. *Blue Letter Bible,* Dictionary and Word Search for *kabowd* (Strong's 3519), 1996-2011, < http://www.blueletterbible.org/lang/lexicon/lexicon.cfm? Strongs=H3519&t=KJV > (accessed May 14, 2011).

3. Biblesoft's New Exhaustive Strong's, s.v. "diabolos," (N.T. 1228).

4. *Blue Letter Bible, Satanas* (Strong's 4567), <http://www.blueletterbible.org/lang/lexicon/lexicon.cfm?Strongs=G4567&t=KJV > (accessed May 14, 2011).

5. *Blue Letter Bible, heylel* (Strong's 1966), <http://www.blueletterbible.org/lang/lexicon/lexicon.cfm?Strongs=H1966&t=KJV > (accessed May 14, 2011).

Bibliography

Booker, Richard. *The End of All Things is at Hand? Are You Ready?* Alachua, FL: Bridge-Logos, 2008.

Booker, Richard. *The Shofar: Ancient Sound of the Messiah.* Houston, TX: Sounds of the Trumpet, Inc., 1999.

Booker, Richard. *Here Comes the Bride: Ancient Jewish Wedding Customs and the Messiah.* Houston, TX: Sounds of the Trumpet Inc., 1995.

Booker, Richard. *Ancient Jewish Prayers and the Messiah.* Houston, TX: Sounds of the Trumpet Inc., 2003.

Charlesworth, James, editor. *The Old Testament Pseudepigrapha: Apocalyptic Literature & Testaments Volume 1.* New York: Doubleday, 1983.

DeMoss, Nancy Leigh, editor. *The Rebirth of America,* Philadelphia: Author S. DeMoss Foundation, 1986.

Fleming, Jim. *Understanding the Revelation.* Bellaire, TX: Biblical Resources, 1999.

Hemer, Colin J. *The Letters to the Seven Churches of Asia in their Local Setting.* Grand Rapids, MI: Eerdmans, 2001.

Ladd, George Eldon. *A Theology of the New Testament*. Grand Rapids, MI: Eerdmans, 1993.

Online Sources: Numerous well-researched articles on Greek mythology and the history, geography and archaeology of the seven cities in Asia Minor.

Osborne, Grant, general editor. *Life Application Bible Commentary: Revelation*. Carol Stream, IL: Tyndale House, 2000.

Wilson, Mark, Arnold, Clinton, editor. *Zondervan Illustrated Bible Backgrounds Commentary: Revelation*. Grand Rapids, MI: Zondervan, 2002.

Tenney, Merrill. *Interpreting Revelation*. Grand Rapids, MI: Eerdmans, 1970.

Stern, David H. *Jewish New Testament Commentary*. Clarksville, MD: Jewish New Testament Publications, 1992.

Varner, William. *Jacob's Dozen: A Prophetic Look at the Tribes of Israel*. Bellmawr, NJ: The Friends of Israel Gospel Ministry, 1987.

Walters, Brent. *Ante-Nicene Christianity: The First Three Centuries*. San Jose, CA: The Ante-Nicene Archive, 1993.

About Dr. Richard Booker

D R. Richard Booker, MBA, Ph.D., is an ordained Christian minister, President of Sounds of the Trumpet, Inc., and the Founder/Director of the Institute for Hebraic-Christian Studies. Prior to entering the ministry, he had a successful business career. He is the author of 35 books, numerous Bible courses, and study materials, which are used by churches and Bible schools around the world.

Dr. Booker has traveled extensively for over 30 years, teaching in churches and at conferences on various aspects of the Christian life as well as Bible prophecy, Israel, and the Hebraic roots of Christianity. He and his wife Peggy have led yearly tour groups to Israel for over 25 years. For 18 years, Dr. Booker was a speaker at the Christian celebration of the Feast of Tabernacles in Jerusalem. This gathering is attended by 5,000 Christians from 100 nations.

Dr. Booker and Peggy founded the Institute for Hebraic-Christian Studies (IHCS) in 1997 as a ministry to educate Christians in the Hebraic culture and background of the Bible, to build relationships between Christians and Jews, and to give comfort and support to the people of Israel. Their tireless work on behalf of Christians and Jews has been recognized around the world, as well as by the Knesset Christian Allies Caucus in Jerusalem.

Dr. Booker is considered a pioneer and spiritual father and prophetic voice in teaching on Bible prophecy, radical Islam, Israel, Jewish-Christian relations, and the biblical Hebraic roots of Christianity. He has made over 400 television programs, which can be seen worldwide on God's Learning Channel. To learn more about his ministry, see his Web site and online bookstore at www.rbooker.com. If you want to invite Dr. Booker to speak at your congregation or conference, you may contact him at shofarprb@aol.com.

In the right hands, This Book will Change Lives!

Most of the people who need this message will not be looking for this book. To change their lives, you need to put a copy of this book in their hands.

> *But others (seeds) fell into good ground, and brought forth fruit, some a hundred-fold, some sixty-fold, some thirty-fold* (Matthew 13:8).

Our ministry is constantly seeking methods to find the good ground, the people who need this anointed message to change their lives. Will you help us reach these people?

> *Remember this—a farmer who plants only a few seeds will get a small crop. But the one who plants generously will get a generous crop* (2 Corinthians 9:6).

EXTEND THIS MINISTRY BY SOWING
3 BOOKS, 5 BOOKS, 10 BOOKS, **OR MORE TODAY,**
AND BECOME A LIFE CHANGER!

Thank you,

Don Nori Sr., Publisher
Destiny Image
Since 1982